FREE

THE INSIDE-OUT GUIDE TO LIFE, UNLIMITED

CLARE DIMOND

CLARE DIMOND

For my Mum, who showed us again and again that, no matter how tough things seem, integrity, love and freedom always shine through.

Thank you Mum.

I love you.

CONTENTS

FOREWORD

In picking up this book you have somehow, whether you know it or not taken notice of a spark that has arisen from deep within. This spark is a flicker from a burning flame of pure love, your true essence, that longs to be recognised. It has never ceased to be yet is often overlooked.

We search for love, for success, for fulfilment, for happiness. The search is never ending because we are looking for them where they cannot be found. All we ever have to do is turn back to the space in which all our experience arises. The space is within us all, our one source. To live from this space knowingly is to be free.

This space of pure and infinite freedom within you is beckoning you back home. It is inviting you to give up the long and tiring pursuit.

It is never the words themselves. It is the pure space of love from which they arise that is the true power.

Every now and then you come across a fellow explorer of truth who points you back home without uttering a single word. Their very presence is shining with love and freedom. They are living from the knowing of who they truly are and it shines through their very being.

This is my experience of the wonderful Clare Dimond. The first time I ever met her I sat in a room of people attending a day long talk by our dear friend and mentor Garret Kramer. Of all the people in the room there was something about Clare. I sensed a presence, a being that shone with love and understanding. The space she points to so astoundingly with her beautiful writing was truly shining from her effortlessly.

It is no wonder that her stunning blog posts and her earlier book REAL have pointed so many back home to this space of constant freedom for which we all long above all else. The words are a pouring out from the heart, from what she has seen and knows within to be true.

Clare is an artist with her words. She paints a picture to be witnessed deep within us all, helping us to see for ourselves who we really are. At the same time her words are so authentic and so relatable to every day life. Her way of sharing this message of freedom, love and understanding is a gift of this lifetime.

When you read this book, let me offer you one small pointer: read as though you are witnessing a beautiful horizon or listening to a stunning piece of classical music. Read from the background space of knowing within you, nothing to remember, no knowledge to intellectually attain. Read from the freedom and love within you from which Clare's words were also written.

It is now time to see beyond all the clouds of thoughts, concepts and beliefs and to pay attention to the one and only source of freedom that has always been within. Because the truth is there is one space of love and freedom, shared by us all. The space from which Clare is pointing is the same space within you that longs to be recognised once again as your true self.

It has always been, and always will be who you are. Now is the time to explore and live a life aligned with this truth.

Enjoy this journey, there is nowhere to get to. Just allow the beautiful pointers in these pages to turn your attention back to the one space that has always remained, here and now. See for yourself what you have always been... FREE.

Grayson Hart

London, England

PROLOGUE

Causeless joy, imperturbable peace, love that knows no opposite and freedom at the heart of all experience....this is your ever-present nature under all circumstances.

Rupert Spira

At first, everything is an adventure. There is so much to explore and see and listen to and do and make and learn and take apart and experience. You reach and crawl and pull yourself up and toddle, investigating your world, awed by the miracles of light and sound and texture around you.

Sometimes you cry and sometimes you laugh. Sometimes you are cross and sometimes you are not. Sometimes you are tired and you sleep and sometimes you are wide awake and ready for adventure. All of life is in you. The world is there for you. You do what is in front of you to do. It is your playground.

Then one day someone gives you a box. It is heavy and you try to put it down but it seems you cannot. "Carry this at all times," says a voice. "It contains the secret to who you really are."

That sounds important. Like something you should know. You try to look in the box but it won't open.

Then another box is put in your hands and the voice says, "This box tells you the secret to finding love."

You realise this secret is important too but that box won't open either.

Then another box is thrust on you. "The secret to happiness." You need to know that secret. Again, the box will not open.

All of a sudden, life appears difficult and complicated. There is a way that you must be in order to have a good life but you can't get into the boxes to find out how. You feel trapped, limited and stuck. You realise it is vital you discover how to open these boxes and find out these secrets. Otherwise what will happen to you? What sort of life will you have?

A final box is handed to you and a voice says,

"This has the secret of freedom."

"Thank goodness," you think, weighed down and worried. "I really need freedom right now". And you try so hard to open that box but the lid is stuck fast.

Now you are fully loaded with the boxes that are getting heavier by the minute.

In the distance you see four huge doors. You hear people laughing and talking behind the doors. Everything sounds amazing, fun and exciting. You want to be part of it.

You try to walk over to the doors but the boxes weigh you down. You know that the secrets to unlocking the doors are in the boxes. You try but the boxes will not open. The life behind the doors sounds like something you will never be part of.

You slump down. You are desperate. "Please help me someone" you cry. And a genie appears before you.

"I can help you," he says. "But first you need to tell me what you know to be true."

You are so confused and low and bewildered. For a long time it has seemed that you don't know anything.

You look in the depths of your being, it seems there is only one thing you know.

"I know these secrets are heavy."

He smiles. "Let me take them from you."

You clutch the boxes tightly to your chest, thinking of Life behind those doors and you shake your head, "I need them."

"Then tell me something else that is true."

There is nothing else. It is hopeless.

He prompts you, "Tell me – have you always had these boxes?"

You look down at one of the boxes. The label on the top says, 'The secret of who you are'. You remember a time when you didn't even know there was a secret. In fact you didn't even think there was a you. You just did what you did and were how you were. There was no trying. There was just being and doing. You realise the simple, unique, perfection of this. The indescribable perfection of you. The lid of the box flies open and in front of you appears a display of the immeasurable diversity of nature. Rainbows, snowflakes, oak trees, daisies, clouds, sunshine, ants, elephants, mountains, diamonds, lions and lambs... all of it glowing with the same shining light. You smile. You get it.

You look at the next box, 'The secret of finding love'. You think back to a time, long ago, when it didn't occur to you that you had to do anything to be loved. You knew you were love. The awareness of this sinks deeper and, as it does, the box gets lighter in your hands. You realise you don't need that secret, have never needed it. There is no secret. The box disappears, and you feel the profound love that you are, have always been.

"What else?" asks the genie.

You look at the box with the secret of happiness. You remember a time when all of life flowed through you, sometimes sad and sometimes happy, sometimes scared and sometimes bold. All of it to be welcomed. All of it to be lived. You realise you are only here to experience life, all of it. You know you don't need that secret. The box turns into a light that bathes you and the ground beneath you feels beyond secure. You feel a profound sense of well-being as you look out towards the horizon with curiosity and peacefulness.

"What else?"

You look at the final box: 'The secret to freedom.' You think back to when you were a small child running, laughing, crying, playing. Pure openness. Pure potential. "I used to be free," you say to the genie, shaking your head sadly. You look at the box expecting it to disappear but it remains as it is. You give it a shake but it stays stuck to your hands.

You frown and look at the genie. He shrugs his shoulders.

You remember the other boxes and you suddenly realise that they were only ever heavy or light, there or not there according to your understanding of who you are. As you saw more clearly, they transformed, disappeared, became something else altogether. You realise with amazement that you have always been free to see this. That you always have been and always will be.

As this insight deepens, you look at the doors again and you can see through them. You see all of life to live, all experience to experience and you realise that somehow you are all of it.

You are the doors, the people, the genie, the boxes and you are no doors, no people, no genie, no boxes.

You are the space in which all of this takes place and does not take place.

There is no line where you end and another begins.

There is nothing and everything.

There is no you and only you.

You are limitless, weightless, infinite.

You are free.

FREE.

FREE

Everyone has experienced that out of nowhere sense of pure ok-ness, pure love, pure freedom in which there is nothing and no one to choose.

Garret Kramer

To be fully alive, fully human, and completely awake is to be continually thrown out of the nest. To live fully is to be always in no-man's-land, to experience each moment as completely new and fresh. To live is to be willing to die over and over again.

Pema Chödrön

PART I
A FRESH LOOK AT FREEDOM

A FRESH LOOK

Honestly, I cannot understand what people mean when they talk about the freedom of the human will.
I have a feeling, for instance, that I will something or other; but what relation this has with freedom I cannot understand at all.
Albert Einstein

This is a book about freedom. About how to live an unlimited life.

You might be reading it because you feel stuck or limited or trapped.

You might know deep inside that there is more that you are capable of but you can't seem to find your way.

You might have fears, concerns or anxieties that you think you should be able to overcome but that seem insurmountable.

You might feel held back by life circumstances, disability, money or education.

You might have narrow limits around your life in order to feel OK. Distances beyond which you cannot travel, people to whom you cannot speak, rituals that must be performed.

You might feel trapped in habits, compulsions or desires that seem to grip you so tightly you feel you will never break free.

I get that. I've felt and believed much of that of myself at different stages and I heard all of it from loved ones, friends, colleagues and clients.

This feeling of being stuck and limited does not sit well with us. It seems to contradict who we are at our very core.

It is therefore an important subject for us to look at more carefully.

Maybe it is the only subject to look at.

Let's begin with how freedom is viewed in our culture. This might be how you see it. It has certainly been how I have seen it.

Freedom is considered something that we have or don't have. That others have or don't have.

Something that, given the right conditions, we might acquire.

Or given adverse conditions, it could be something that we lose, that decreases in scope, accessibility. It is therefore something to hold on to and defend.

It looks like it is made possible or limited by our talent, education, character, wealth, physical ability, connections, mental health.

We can live with a sense of never quite getting there. Blaming ourselves that we don't have the freedom that our education, the circumstances of our upbringing, our intelligence should bring about.

Or we can feel limited by our background, our lack of contacts or confidence or our health and believe we have very little ability to steer our desired course in life.

It looks like it is only possible by diligently securing and managing ourself, our choices and the world.

Freedom.

Something fixed, out there, to strive for, to give up on, to be allowed or denied, to protect and defend, to judge ourselves against, to worry about losing.

That doesn't sound very free. That doesn't sound much like freedom.

And it doesn't sound much like freedom because there is no freedom in it.

And there is no truth in it either.

This book is an exploration of what is true about the boundaries that we believe limit us and our lives. It is about how when we see more clearly who we are we realise not just that we have unlimited freedom, but that *freedom is who we are.*

This book is about the idea of a limited self and a restricted world that thought and belief continually create. It is about how, when we get wise to that, we can live in reality. We realise our true nature.

There is more freedom available than you could have ever possibly imagined. There is an existence that is right here for you, waiting for you to take it up and live, in which it is impossible for you to imagine what a limit or a restriction could even be.

There is only one truth in this book.

The truth is that you are freedom. You are freedom itself. Unlimited, unbounded. Pure potential. Pure freedom.

It is just sometimes you believe otherwise.

That's it. It is no more complicated than that.

But oh my goodness how hard it can be sometimes to see that. How hard it can be to see that when it looks like we are being so firmly held back by a lack of money, qualifications, support and other resources and trapped by responsibilities, commitments and demands on our time and energy.

The idea that you are freedom itself might sound ridiculous right now. It might well be opposite to everything you have ever believed about who you are, about the things that seem to get in your way, about the nature of choice, action and doing.

My own search to see something more clearly about who I was and how I could live more freely lasted decades.

Then, thanks to a mind-blowing book called *The Inside Out Revolution*, by Michael Neill, I found out about an understanding articulated by a gentleman named Sydney Banks. Sometimes called the Three Principles, the Inside-Out Understanding or Subtractive Psychology, it describes how reality is created in ever-changing thought and that there is deeper more constant substance to who we are. That this deeper constant substance is love, intelligence, awareness, freedom.

This seemed brand-new, ground-breaking and at the same something we have known forever. It chimed with words of the great sages, philosophers, scientists and writers throughout the ages.

As I explored this understanding further, every aspect of life changed. At the heart of this change are some crazy, ridiculous but simple principles.

That we are not what we think we are and the world is not what we think it is.

That thought and experience of who we are and what the world is change all the time.

That we have the capacity to be aware of this transient thought-created idea of self and other.

That awareness itself, the fact of being aware, not the content, is who we really are.

So what does this have to do with freedom?

Well, I had been told, maybe you were too—and I believed, maybe you did too—that freedom comes from money, other people, having a better boss or a different job or a different body, being more assertive or go-getting, making better choices, working harder.

You might, like me, have spent a lifetime searching for freedom in this way.

But here's the thing . . .

Freedom doesn't come from work, money, qualifications, other people, health or changes in lifestyle.

Freedom doesn't even come from a better state of mind or more positive thoughts or better ideas or a more can-do attitude.

It doesn't even come from leaving prison or an abusive relationship or unemployment or any other thing we see as trapping us.

Freedom doesn't come from a different personality.

Freedom doesn't come from changing anything about ourselves or the world we see around us.

Freedom comes from seeing who we are.

Freedom is who we are before we believe the idea of a limited self.

That's it.

And all the measures we are taking to try to increase our freedom, if they are pointing us in any other direction than the unlimited nature of who we really are, are keeping us in the belief that we are stuck.

The irony is, when we start to see this, we realise there is nothing, not one single thing, that we need to resist or change.

And even more ironically, this loving openness, connectedness and clear sightedness is the only basis for true, lasting change.

To live life from that clarity and understanding is what we are talking about in this book.

It is the only space in which the realisation of the freedom of our true nature is possible.

And for many of us, much of the time, it really doesn't look like it.

To see it more clearly, we need to turn the whole damn thing, everything that we think about freedom, on its head…

You are freedom (and sometimes you believe you are not)

HIDING IN PLAIN SIGHT

I wished to know the meaning of things.
I am the meaning.
I wished to find a warrant for being.
I need no warrant for being, and no word of sanction upon my being.
I am the warrant and the sanction.
Ayn Rand

You are riding on a horse, looking for the horse.
Ajahn Chah

In one of his typically disturbing Tales of the Unexpected, renowned author Roald Dahl tells the story of a pregnant woman whose husband announces he wants a divorce. Overcome with fear and anger, she hits him over the head with the frozen leg of lamb she had on the counter to prepare for lunch. The husband dies instantly. She panics thinking of her unborn child and wonders desperately how she can escape detection. She puts the leg of lamb in the oven to destroy the evidence and then goes to the grocers to create an alibi.

On her return, she calls the police and tells them that someone has murdered her husband. They arrive at the house and comment on the delicious smell of roast lamb. She invites them to join her for lunch and they readily agree. They sit around her dining table, eating the lamb and talking about the critical importance of finding the murder weapon...

This (minus the murder and the leg of lamb and the police) is exactly the challenge with realising the freedom of our true nature. It is right there under our noses. We have it already. We are living it, eating it, wearing it, saying it, doing it.

But because we don't realise this, we spend our time looking for it. Not only that but we are looking for something that has nothing to do with what freedom actually is, in the place where it cannot possibly be found. It is this misunderstanding, this quest that makes it impossible to find.

But for all of us, once we understand what freedom really means, the search is over. We can no longer exhaust ourselves in looking high and low for something that we already have in infinite quantity.

What is going on? Why do so many of us believe ourselves to be trapped and limited? Why does freedom seem so hard to find?

The reason we can't find it is because we are trying to find it in more and better choices, in having the money, qualifications and resources that will set us free, in being a freer, less restricted version of ourselves. We don't realise how believing that freedom lies in these, takes us further away from realising the freedom of our true nature.

The origins of this misunderstanding lie in:

- our belief that we are who we think we are
- our belief that we are separate from objects, others and circumstances
- our belief that we have free choice

Now you might look at those three beliefs and think,

'What the hell is she talking about?

Of course I am who I think I am.

Of course I'm completely separate from that person over there.

Of course I decide what I do.'

And that is completely logical, understandable and natural because that is how it looks. Yet, when we start exploring all three more closely it becomes very obvious that how things look to us, how we believe them to be, can never be how they actually are.

When we play hide and seek at home, my daughter will sit on the chair under which my son is hiding, shaking her head and saying 'maybe he's in the bedroom, Mum'. It is the same with freedom. Thought will tell us freedom is hiding elsewhere, that we haven't found it when we have it right here and right now. Even the slightest glimpse into what is actually happening rocks the world as we know it to be.

In the next chapters we will look at each belief more closely and start to see the real freedom it obscures.

THE FREEDOM OF NO SELF

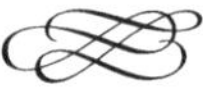

The biggest ego trip going is trying to get rid of your ego. And the joke of it all is that the ego doesn't exist.
Alan Watts

I am nobody.
Who are you?
Are you nobody too?
Emily Dickinson

You might have expected this book to advise on how we can improve ourselves to gain more freedom. Become the sort of person that overcomes obstacles. That has a thicker skin or no fear or is more assertive or decisive. Recommend how we can 'get out of our own way' to have more of what we want. How we can have stronger belief in ourselves.

We won't be doing that.

In fact we'll be doing the opposite.

Because it is in the moments that we believe that we need to be different and that the world has to change for us to be ok, that we cannot experience freedom.

This is because these thoughts and beliefs are hand-me-downs. They come from a life of conditioning, from being told and innocently believing what we are and what is needed to be secure, loved, happy. It is these beliefs themselves that stop us seeing the ultimate freedom at the heart of our being.

Let's take a good look at this person that wants freedom, that apparently bought this book. Because everything we believe about this person, this 'I', is hiding the unlimited, absolute, infinite freedom of our existence right here and now in this exact minute.

This 'I' of ours—called, among other things, me, myself, who I am, ego, identity, sense of self—is an idea created in thought.

And if that sounds ridiculous, take a moment (or perhaps a life-time, there's no rush) to reflect on how everything we think about our lives, our personality, our flaws, our talent, our body, our entire selves is always thought, thought that happens to be believed in the moment. All of it subject to change as the state of mind changes. None of it fixed. None of it true.

This idea of who we are and whether we think we are capable or need to improve has nothing complete or objective in it. What I think right now about who I am is a momentary creation of thought believed. It will change. (For a more detailed exploration of who we really are, see the book *REAL: The inside-out guide to being yourself.*)

Any belief will, by its nature, define and separate and say

'this' but not 'that. Any belief, therefore, is a limiting belief. A belief by definition must pin down and restrict. It cannot liberate.

Even those freedom mantras that we chant into the bathroom mirror (Or maybe that was just me? Probably the mantra dancing was just me.):

'I can do anything.'

'I have all the resources in the world.'

'I have unlimited power.'

'I am free to do what I want.'

Even those, even if actually believed, would pin us down and restrict us, because all of them are based on an idea of ourselves as a distinct, separate, fixed individual. They are based on the idea that what we think we are is what we are.

But thoughts come and go. They change all the time. They look 100% real in the moment but there is no substance to them. As long as we are believing what we think about ourselves, our understanding of self depends entirely on whatever thoughts appear, out of the blue, into awareness.

And this creates a weird set up because it means that there is no freedom in this idea of self. There is no freedom because the instant the thought of an I is believed we are suddenly held fast. Fixed in this belief of self with all its apparent, incumbent, believed-to-be-true physical and mental limits.

Indeed this self only exists because of limits. The boundaries of the body. The limitations of personality and fears. The restrictions of lifestyle, income, education. The separation between self and other. The distinctions and comparisons. The 'this' but 'not this'.

Not one of these limits even exists until the thought of 'I' arises. Then suddenly, with the single thought 'I', other thoughts of a world in relation to that I, appear and take shape, look real, seem significant, important, insurmountable.

The only time we experience the pure freedom that we really are is in the moment that the 'I' does not exist. In the moment of no self reference, no self awareness—and therefore no self—there is total unrestricted freedom. There is being and doing that seems to come from the pure freedom of life itself.

And if this sounds like some quest that will have you chanting your way barefoot across the Himalayas until finally, in a cave full of goat shit, you suddenly find enlightenment, worry not.

You have this experience of no 'I' much of the time.

You just don't notice it because in those moments there is no thought of 'I' to record it and analyse it and judge it. You might even have been in a state of absorption without any self reference reading this. (You might not of course. You might have been reading so far thinking '*I* am outraged by this. Why did *I* waste my money on such rubbish.' In which case, please don't leave a review just yet.)

We have the experience of no 'I' when we are so absorbed in simply being or doing that we are transported out of the bounds of our idea of self.

Some of these moments become the stuff of news headlines. Like the mother picking up a car to rescue a child trapped beneath its wheels, the athlete running the race of his or her life, the scientist accessing the previously inaccessible, the author taking readers to the furthest corners of the imagination, an entire stadium of people, breathless in wonder at a transcending guitar solo or a soaring vocal.

Some are so prosaic, ubiquitous and familiar that we don't even consider the pure freedom that they represent. The crawling baby achieving the impossible and pulling itself up. A child and a bike and feet off the ground. The momentary, wonder on a walk in the hills or by the sea or as we look at the night sky. The disappearance of self as we make love or laugh or sing or write or do the washing up.

In that moment of self-dissolved absorption in life, there is no thought about limit on our capacity. In that moment we are set free of what has gone before, of our conditioned life, of what we think we can do, of who we think we are.

We experience the no 'I' in moments of pure love or mind blowing marvel or in a knowing that reaches beyond thought. Those are the moments when we are in touch with the absolute freedom at the heart of our existence.

My dear friend, colleague and author of the foreword to this book, Grayson Hart, is a professional rugby player as well as a coach and speaker. He describes moments when he is so immersed in the game that there is no self awareness. He is simply movement, so in tune with the play and the field and the players that anything is possible.

He compares this to the times when it looked like it mattered how well he played, that his well-being, future or salary depended on it. He would run onto the pitch with a head full of self-judgement. Fully self-conscious, all he could experience in those moments were the limits of the self.

I think of my son and daughter as babies training their fresh new eyes to look at me or bringing a wobbling arm to reach for my face. There was no thought in their minds of 'should' or 'must'. There was no thought of how they would look or that it mattered that they could gaze for longer than a second or grasp my necklace. They were simply a miracle of a body, infused with life, learning and mind-blowing resolve. Doing what had been, right up until that moment, impossible with no thought of an 'I' to tell them no.

I think of how I write. Sometimes I cease to exist and all I am is a means for words to reach a page. They come from nowhere, they take form, they transpose themselves to the page. There is pure freedom in this. And then there are moments when I worry about how the writing will be perceived, whether people will criticise me and ridicule me. Instantly I am plunged into an idea of who I am, a self that needs to get things right and my sense of freedom evaporates.

The experience of freedom is our true nature. We know this. And the unease when we feel trapped or constrained tells us that something is amiss.

We can go in search of freedom as something to acquire or to achieve through deliberate obliteration of thought. We can use substances and activity to wipe out the mental self references. We drink or take drugs or shop or eat to try to switch off the running commentary of the apparently limited self. But these are temporary fixes. Soon this idea of 'I' reappears loud and clear, thoughts full of self blame, self loathing are believed. And the cycle begins again.

When we use something to find our freedom, we are looking in the wrong direction. It looks like freedom has to be won, bought in, fought for. There is no end to this fruitless quest. The search takes us away from our true nature, the only place where freedom can be found.

Deep down we know that there is nothing to do or change, that we are freedom itself. It is just that sometimes we forget it. The forgetting is perfect because it is this which allows us to realise who we really are.

All of us know the freedom at the heart of our being. The liberation of realising we are so much more than we think.

We recognise those moments of freedom, of simply being and doing with no judgement, no critique, no comparison, no defence, no future projection or past reference.

We know that our nature is freedom and we know this is why it never feels authentic living a restricted, illusory idea of who we are.

THE FREEDOM OF NO SELF.

THE FREEDOM OF NO SEPARATION

Give your attention to the experience of seeing rather than to the object seen and you will find yourself everywhere.
Rupert Spira

When we feel trapped and we want to find a way to have more freedom, we look at the things, people and circumstances that are holding us back or getting in our way.

Let's have a look at these things that seem to be in the way or that we think we need. And, to start this off, let's have a look at how all of these are experienced.

The fact is that everything is experienced through thought. In other words, objects appear and disappear in consciousness. Without the perception there is no object.

The world that looks so real is actually a creation of perception brought alive in awareness.

And, yes, I know, this sounds like total nonsense.

Because, of course, there are things that exist independently of thought. Real things like furniture, trees, money, taxes, marriage, jobs, birth, death . . . Regardless of what I "think" about my laptop, I still need it to write this book and if it stops working it will cause me a problem. If my car breaks down and I can't get to an interview then inevitably I will be at a disadvantage. The breakdown will be limiting my freedom, directly.

These things look completely separate from me. Nothing to do with thought. Just simple cause and effect.

Well actually no.

Because there is no experience that isn't created by perception in the moment, that doesn't exist other than through the medium of thought brought alive in consciousness. Everything appears in some way, therefore, as a function of belief, attention and thought.

And if we don't see this, then that is only because we don't see it, not because it isn't true. A helium balloon or a candle flame could look like they are defying gravity. But . . . nope. They just show us again how gravity works.

How can it be that things that look so objective and separate from us are not?

Let's start with something easy.

Let's all consider a table we are familiar with. What's yours like? My table is real and not imaginary. So might yours be. If I were to walk straight into my table, I would bang my leg. It might be the same with yours. Mine is here in my life. No amount of contemplating the nature of thought, even on an intensive retreat where no one wears clothes and we all eat strange herbs, is going to make it not real. It is a real table. It is really there.

There are many moments when this table is simply useful. Like now. Using it to write this book. Very handy. There are moments when it is clear of clutter, shining, clean and seems to make me really happy

There are many moments when the table doesn't even cross my mind. For example, I only occasionally think about my table when I am out with friends (Joking of course! I often think about it. No, really, I rarely think about it when I am out. Maybe even never. Honestly . . .)

There are also many moments when it seems to cause me stress. Sometimes I look at the remnants of a previous meal or the piles of bills upon it as clear indications that my life is falling apart, and how on earth can I coach people when I don't even have a clean, uncluttered table?

A table has the power to be useful, to make me happy or to turn me into a failure and hypocrite. Wow. That is some table that can do all that. Except it can't. It has no superpowers. It has no ability to infiltrate my mind and make me happy, grateful, insecure, stressed.

Thoughts on the other hand . . . They have all the superpowers in the world. They create the idea of people coming in, seeing the remains of dinner still uncleared, the disorganized bills, and then silently judging. They create the idea of a person who is not on top of her life and the feelings of shame or inadequacy.

It is truly amazing what thought can do. The panoramic, 4D, incredible special-effects film that is produced out of nowhere in a split second. And we attribute it so innocently, and so completely misguidedly, to something outside us, that looks absolutely separate. The table is making me stressed. The table is making me happy. The table is making me sad. It looks like this is cause and effect, something objective and independent of perception is causing feeling.

None of this can possibly be true.

And just as it is not true of the table, so it is not true of the computer, the broken down car, the weather, the interview clothes, the train timetable, the pile of work to do, the house, the bank balance….

Let's take another real aspect of this table. Suppose I were to bang my foot on it. It is solid and real and so my foot cannot pass through it. I can bang my foot on it. The collision between foot and table is real. The pain would be felt. Surely that is real and nothing to do with thought?

Well everything about that collision and pain (indeed whether the collision and pain is even noticed and therefore whether in that moment they exist or not) is an experience in consciousness.

It could be:

"Damn me for being so clumsy!"

"Damn this table for being in the way, and also for being so dirty and piled up with papers!"

"Pain! How cool! My nerve endings are working. I am a walking miracle!"

"What? Oh, yes, a broken toe possibly. But look at this awesome manicure I got today . . ."

Or nothing at all, no collision noted, no pain felt. So collision and pain do not exist within that experience.

Or an infinite array of other possibilities in the moment.

All these experiences have their own movie—blame, gratitude, guilt, wonder, distraction—which have zero to do with tables, zero to do with pain, and everything to do with the infinitely creative power of thought brought alive in awareness in the moment. It's amazing isn't it?

And there's another way we can consider this.

This table looks to me like something made of wood, designed to put things on. That's the reality of the table for me, the shorthand of it. To my 6-year-old, it is a shelter for Lego wars. To my 11-year-old, it creates a cosy corner in which to watch dance videos. To a quantum scientist, it would be mostly empty space. To an upcycler, it could be a chair or a crib or anything else. To an inhabitant of a dystopian wasteland, it would be firewood or a weapon.

There is no limit to how the table can be considered. There is no limit to how much there is to find out about it. There is no limit to the layers of understanding of it or to the things that imagination could create with it. There is no limit to how present it appears or to how it can not appear at all. All of this is experienced and created through the mind, through thought believed.

As it is with the table, so it is (now and ever shall be) with EVERYTHING else.

Even the stuff that looks real and solid and objective. Money, taxes, trees, marriage, birth, death, laptops, broken down cars, even ourselves . . . all of them are real, but, like the table, all of them exist or don't exist, are one thing or another, are simple or complex, awful or wonderful or anything in between according to thought in the moment.

Experience is generated through thought believed. A state-of-the-art special-effects department brings these thoughts about self and other alive to such an extent that they are experienced physically and mentally as a separate reality.

And let's be really clear. This is not about positive thinking or mind management or controlling thoughts or seeing the silver lining.

It is simply about noticing the incredible power of thought to conjure up an experience, an entire "reality" in any one moment. It is true of the table. It is true of every experience we ever have including experience of self.

To see this makes all the difference in the world.

We start to become clearer, more aware that the only reliable constant in all this is awareness itself. We become more insightful about the nature of experience and the nature of who we believe ourselves to be. We start to realise that nothing is separate from us. All of it is appearing and disappearing in the awareness that somehow we are making possible.

When we find ourselves stuck with an internal movie about a certain thing—for example, "I can't work without a computer"; or, "I'm such a failure. I can't even drive to the interview"; or, "I need money to do what I want to do."—we can realise that the only ultimate truth is that we are aware of the experience of a limited self and a limiting reality. All of it brought into existence through the creative power of thought, all of it insubstantial and transient.

The apparent world of self separate from other does not exist in any real sense other than through transient experience, through thought arising in consciousness.

And this realisation draws us easily and simply into reality. A reality in which it looks like there is a table there, for sure, but in which we are the awareness that the entire experience of that table is created through thought in the moment.

As we come into this reality, we move free of the illusion we were trapped in; we start to see things differently. Each moment becomes animated with the ultimate truth that we are a space in which thoughts and beliefs turn into form.

Realising this to even a tiny extent is a breakthrough. It is a sliver of reality and truth. It allows us to have a new, more accurate perspective on who we really are. We no longer take experience as a representation of reality, as information. We start looking towards something more stable and true. We increasingly make the distinction between the impermanent, ever-changing and fluctuating nature of experience and the permanent, unchanging and constant factors of human existence.

As we see this, it no longer makes sense to find freedom by controlling a world of seemingly separate objects.

It makes real sense to find freedom by looking within to the origin of that world. By looking to our understanding that everything is an experience within awareness. That somehow the awareness we are is making all of it possible.

THE FREEDOM OF NO SEPARATION

THE FREEDOM OF NO CHOICE

You can do what you decide to do — but you cannot decide what you will decide to do.
Sam Harris, Free Will

The idea of choice is only an option available in thought. Consciousness knows no choice. It's complete. One.
Grayson Hart

You maintain that you are free to take either the right- or the left-hand fork in the road. I defy you to set up a single objective criterion by which you can prove after you have made the turn that you might have made the other.
Percy Williams Bridgman, The Nature of Physical Theory

What a confusing title to this chapter. How can there be freedom in no choice?

Isn't freedom only ever about being able to choose to do or have or say or write anything or go anywhere we want?

It looks like our life is made up of choices.

It looks like the more choices available to us the more free we are.

The more able we are to go after exactly what we want—the job, the salary, the car, the holiday, the lifestyle, the partner—the more freedom we have.

Well, let's look at choice for a moment.

All day, every day it looks like we are making choices:

Cereal or toast for breakfast? (If you are in the UK. Fish or tofu if you are in Japan. Netflix or youtube if you are my children. But don't tell anyone that).

Exercise or not?

Train to work or drive?

Emails or chat to colleagues?

Lunch in or out?

Finish the work or leave it for tomorrow?

Out in the evening or watch tv?

Bed now or later?

All of these choices look absolutely real. Indeed for many of them it might look that we are trapped in one particular option. 'I have to get up now because…', 'I have to work because…' 'I have to/I must/I should...'

And in between them are more apparent choices, infinite choices, that when we consider them look just as real.

And it looks to us that our success, the fulfilment of our potential, our eventual happiness, our freedom lie within the code of these micro and macro choices.

When it looks like we are failing it must be because of the wrong choices we have made and are making. When it looks like we are doing well it seems like we are making right decisions.

When it looks like we are stuck or trapped it looks like we have no choice about what we do. Or it looks like none of the choices available to us are what we want.

Every time we think of ourselves, this is what we are faced with. An apparently real person, real world, real objects, real other people and real tasks. And all of this looks like it has to be navigated through decision after decision, limit after limit in order for us to have more of the good times and less of the bad.

When we think of our freedom from this perspective it looks like there is effort we can put in, states of mind and thinking that we can foster, needs we can satisfy in order to lead a freer, happier, more fulfilling life. And all of this seems to take place within a world of constraints and limits. Limited by our background, resources and character we try to find freedom in a world of limited choice and resources.

So on the one hand it looks like we are an individual with the capacity for free will. And on the other hand it looks like there are very real constraints, either personal or in the world, that limit that free will.

Our civilisation is underpinned by this principle. Our judicial and penal system. Our food industry. Our medical and education system. The way we bring up our kids and the way we congratulate or blame ourselves.

We believe we are individuals with free will and the power to steer our lives through the good and bad choices we make. We also believe we are limited by things outside our control.

Well in this chapter we will look at how that cannot possibly be true.

And I'm going to add one more crazy statement into the mix:

IN THE MOMENTS WHEN WE BELIEVE WE ARE AN INDIVIDUAL WITH THE FREEDOM TO CHOOSE, WE CANNOT REALISE OUR FREEDOM.

And I can hear the sound of books slamming shut and e-readers clicking off and the zero star reviews on Amazon going up. *Because, Jeez, we just want to know how to have the resources and options to get more freedom. We don't need it to get all heavy and confusing.*

Stay with this a bit longer, because, I promise you, the only genuine freedom lies in seeing that, from the 'reality' of a deciding separate self, no choice and no freedom is ever possible.

Let's consider our experience.

We do something. Eat a slice of cake perhaps. And it looks as though we decided, freely, to do it. It seems that we are a free agent, making our own way through the world.

But that cannot be true.

A thought comes to mind. (Who or what determines which thought come to mind?) We believe it or not. (What decides which thoughts are believed?) Or another thought comes to mind that gives a different option. Two thoughts, appearing out of the blue, saying two different things. Eat the cake. Don't eat the cake.

It looks like we are making a choice, acting on our free will. But all that has happened is that two thoughts have arrived. Both from nowhere. Both out of our control. Both appearing within awareness. One of them, 'Eat the cake' perhaps (if you are like me), seems to win against the other. The reasons why this thought would trump the 'Don't eat the cake' thought are not visible to us.

Who knows where these thoughts come from? Who knows how one thought rather than another from this infinite melting pot of information seems more believable? There is no transparency of any of the behind the scenes stuff. One moment—no thought about cake. The next moment—thought about cake.

Sam Harris, author of 'Free Will' says, "Your brain is making choices on the basis of preferences and beliefs that have been hammered into it over a lifetime - by your genes, your physical development since the moment you were conceived, and the interactions you have had with other people, events, and ideas. Where is the freedom in this? Yes, you are free to do what you want even now. But where did your desires come from?"

Where is the freedom in that?

There is none.

It looks like we are doing what we want. Eating the cake. It is presented as a freedom. But when we consider that the thoughts that come to mind appear and are believed without any transparency, acting on them can logically only be about limitation. Believing our thoughts, we are pinned by the mind, by unconscious processes, by the weight of our conditioning and beliefs.

And we call this freedom.

And even more intriguing are the many neurological studies, such as those carried out by Benjamin Libet, that show that neural activity towards an action initiates as much as 10 seconds before we are consciously aware of a decision to act.

In other words, there is evidence that the act is initiated and then thoughts appear to make out it was a free decision.

This is our apparent conscious control over our life. In which it looks like we see the stimulus, assess it and then, with freedom and free will, respond.

But as far as free will is concerned, at worst, our actions are launched before any conscious awareness whatsoever.

At best, our actions are decided by whichever conscious thought (of which the timing, content and format is governed by some process about which we have no idea) seems (for reasons completely out of our awareness) most believable.

Where is the free will in that?

And yet it looks absolutely as though we are a real individual actively making a free choice. And accordingly we attribute blame to self and other for 'wrong' choices and praise for 'right' ones. It is impossible in those moments in which we see ourselves as separate and individual to conceive that who we believe we are is not choosing. As the writer Isaac B Singer cleverly says, 'We must believe in free will. We have no choice.'

But as we start exploring the nature of thought and consciousness more carefully, it becomes more and more obvious that every experience of this apparent self is only ever thought believed from moment to moment.

And it becomes obvious that just as this apparent self is created from thoughts believed, so is everything believed about decisions and choices. So is everything believed about limits and constraints.

The essential element of this experience of self, options, decision and limits is that ALL OF IT IS CREATED IN THOUGHT.

The whole entire thing - the idea of self, choices - is all created out of thought that changes from moment to moment. All of it can disappear, reappear, turn into something else with the next thought.

In any moment that we believe this thought-created experience we are temporarily stuck with a belief about who we are and what is important. We experience a lack of freedom because in that moment we can't see that we are the space in which all these thoughts arise. We can't see that we are freedom itself.

"I am no bird; and no net ensnares me: I am a free human being with an independent will." said Charlotte Brontë's Jane Eyre. And as long as we continue to believe this we are trapped, with no experience of genuine freedom whatsoever.

We are constrained within a world of reactions and responses.

We are limited by made up alternatives that look real but which only ever exist as creations of thought.

We see limits and boundaries and constraints that only ever exist in the way they are perceived.

We are trapped in a limited idea of self, itself created in thought, that experiences apparently real choices, all of which are created in thought. All of it transient, insubstantial.

Freedom has nothing to do with the choices we apparently make.

So where is the freedom then if it does not lie in choice? How do we move beyond our conditioned thoughts, beliefs and reactions?

This is where it gets so fascinating and exciting. This is where life completely transforms.

Because if our whole experience of self, life and other is created in thought then any insight, even the slightest glimpse, into the nature of thought and into what we are beyond will inevitably shift reality.

And what are we if we are not the content of thought? We must be the space in which thought arises and is believed. Awareness is the only constant. Awareness is the only non-changing, stable, reliable aspect of our whole experience of life.

Freedom from the patterns, beliefs and limits lies in realising we are the space in which they appear. Anything that points us in this direction, that allows us to hang out in this space takes us closer and closer to the reality of who we are.

And what is this reality? What is the nature of this awareness? How do we know when we are caught up believing transient thought and when we are in the freedom of seeing who we really are?

My coach Garret Kramer once wrote one of the clearest pointers to this:

Any feeling, emotion, judgement, idea, concept or theory that comes from your ability to think (given that it's subject to change) is not

true. Love is the only thing that doesn't come from your ability to think.
Love is the only thing that's true.

It is that simple.

When we act, move, speak, write, run, play from purest love, we are free.

Free of all the ideas and concepts, the beliefs and thoughts about who we should be. Free of an insecure self that needs the world to be a certain way. Free of believing that we are somehow unconnected and separate from the world around us. Free of conditioning and beliefs handed down to us by generation upon generation.

As Marianne Williamson said, "From a mind filled with infinite love comes the power to create infinite possibilities".

The thoughts, ideas, fears and insecurities might still be there. They might still look real. But coming from love, we glide through them all and we watch them disappear in the light of our presence.

And we are not talking conditional love here. We are not talking about the games that thoughts play. The seeking that fixes on an object or person and says 'I need this to be OK'. The type of love that, in Shakespeare's words, 'alters when it alteration finds'.

We are talking about something quite different. We are talking about what Emily Dickinson describes as 'anterior to life, posterior to death, initial of creation, and the exponent of breath'.

We are talking about that feeling deep in the centre of our

being, that space of knowing, that freedom of seeing it all, allowing it all. That settled feeling of truth, constancy.

We feel the perfection, the rightness of it, the fit of it. It has nothing to do with decisions or outcomes or need or resistance. We move way beyond the limits of choice, beyond ideas of self and other. And we know that this is who we are.

THE FREEDOM OF NO CHOICE

WHAT NOW?

Freeing yourself was one thing,
claiming ownership of that freed self was another.
Toni Morrison, Beloved

And now comes the big question - how do we get to live from this place of no 'I' and no separation? How do we move to the place before thoughts pile in and create a limited self and world.

How do we live our freedom?

It's a great question and an impossible one.

Because it is not possible to get to the no 'I' from the perspective of the 'I'.

It is impossible to realise that there is no separation when we are looking at a whole world apparently separate from us.

It is impossible to move beyond choice when faced with apparent choices.

It is impossible to realise the truth of who we are when we are seeking anything other than what is right now.

It would be like James Bond wiping off a mark on the screen on which Diamonds are Forever is showing (thank you to my teacher Garret Kramer for that analogy).

It would be like the woman, seeing her child beneath the wheels of a car, trying to convince herself that she has the physical strength and resolve to pick up the car.

It would be like the athlete, evaluating ways that she can be a better runner as she tried to run the race of her life.

It would be like the author trying to impress his readers with his brilliance.

It would be the crawling baby thinking he should be walking by now.

It would be like you, living your already perfect life, thinking you should be living it in a different way.

It would be like you, being the indefinable essence of life and being you already are, thinking you should be something else.

It would be like you, already free, believing you have to do something to be free.

Self-consciousness cannot experience freedom. And the search to free ourselves can only ever create more self-consciousness.

The harder we try to free ourselves from the 'I', the more we seem to make this 'I', which does not exist other than in thought, a thing.

Cats sit on the lap of the person in the room that most hates cats. Wasps buzz around the face of the person who makes the most fuss about wasps. (I know that because of my husband and my sister.)

The more we resist (the self, the cat, the wasp, the anything), the more it seems an issue. The more it seems to persist.

The more I tried to get rid of a public speaking phobia, the more real the phobia and this self that had a problem seemed to become.

It is exactly the same with freedom.

Freedom is ours when we know it matters not one jot whether we are aware of being free or not. When we know that the flow between the limits of self-consciousness and the freedom of simply being alive is as natural as the movement from night to day. Neither one better than the other.

Like a dream that we try to recall on wakening, or the name that we have forgotten, it is the striving and seeking freedom that chases it out of awareness.

Seeing this more clearly marks the beginning and the end of our relentless pursuit. It marks the end of our continuous resistance to what is.

Whenever we are looking for something or someone that we believe will bring security, love or freedom, we can be sure we are believing an idea of who we are and in that moment of seeking it is impossible to experience the security, love and freedom that already lies beneath the thoughts and beliefs. Freedom is not to be found by a limited idea of self, created from thought, in a limited world, also created from thought. And it is not to be found in trying to escape this either.

We move between seeing our soaring true capacity, our

limitless space, our excellence, our openness to all experience and being seemingly plunged back into the limits of pedestrian seeking and resistance.

And that is perfect. That is how life is - moments of pure life and moments of believing the commentary on life. That will always happen. We don't need to change any of it.

Freedom lies in seeing the perfection of this.

Any book, teacher or course that points you in any other direction is pointing you towards trying to fight illusory limits and ultimately more suffering.

And I really know that this is not easy to get our heads around. It is so opposite to the way we have been brought up to see the world and ourselves.

But as we see more and more clearly who we are, the misunderstanding loses its grip. The apparent separation between ourselves, the world and our potential becomes more obviously illusory. We realise what we are, what we have always been, pure life living itself, pure potential realising itself. We also realise that it is our nature to forget this.

We suffer when we forget who we are and when we forget that it is the most natural thing in the world to forget!

Freedom is the background knowledge that however it looks, however we are suffering, however trapped we seem, ultimately, we, as the space in which this experience of suffering and constraint occurs, are free.

THE FREEDOM OF WHO WE REALLY ARE

PART II
LIFE, UNLIMITED

The privilege of a lifetime is to become who you truly are.
Carl Jung

WHAT ABOUT THE REAL STUFF?

We are identifying with what is passing, so fear comes. We are trying to make steady and permanent what is by nature impermanent.
Mooji

Hopefully you are getting an idea that the thought-created idea of self appears and disappears. That we are the space in which this takes place. And that our freedom lies in seeing this more clearly.

If you are like me though there may still be some enormous objections.

'Well let's get real for a second. Let's come back to real life for a moment. Because there are real, actually real things that make some people more stuck and limited than others...'

There are so many things out there in the world that seem to be firmly planted between us and what we could do if we had more freedom. Things like other people, and life circumstances, money, time. Things like the events of our past that mean we are now a certain way, on a certain path, heading towards a certain future.

Then to add into the mix are all the elements about ourselves that seem to hold us back. Things like our lack of motivation, our health, the overload of work that we struggle with, our personality and our flaws, the limits of our talent and ability.

When we think about our freedom and whether we are living life to the full, it is very easy to create a long list of people, circumstances, events that are blocking us now or that have blocked us in the past or which we can see will block us in the future.

These all look like real issues and obstructions that must be dealt with in order for us to be free.

And from this perspective it might look like we have the delusion of freedom until the real world of limits intervenes and we come back down to earth with a bump, forced to face up to responsibilities and burdens.

So is that it? Is that what life is?

Moments of blissful, head in the sand ignorance until the harsh reality of life crashes in and we are forced to face our limits and restrictions?

No. The opposite is true.

Our true existence is permanent, complete, unlimited freedom. That is our nature. It is just that we have moments (and for some of us there are very many of these moments) when we forget. We have moments when it seems without any doubt that we are restricted and bound in. That we do not have the resources, and never will, to live truthfully and fully.

These are moments when we forget who we really are. When

it looks like the limits we see around us are actually able to somehow stop the love, creativity and intelligence that we are here to express.

And we know it is this way round because we know that every single experience of self, responsibility, limit or obstacle is an experience of thought believed. Without that thought believed, there is nothing.

The experience of these 'limits' is real. The feelings of frustration or anxiety or stuckness are real.

But occasionally we see glimpses that there is no fixed, permanent world out there to limit us. That the content of experience is not fixed or permanent or objective. That there is no fixed, permanent self to be limited. That it is impossible for the experience to be independent of the perceiver.

Perhaps you might have already noticed how one moment a situation looks real and terrible, then perhaps real and manageable, then perhaps real and perfect and then perhaps not real or not even relevant. And everything in between.

We will see how this realisation means that the limits of our fears, conditioning, beliefs and concerns no matter how deeply ingrained start to weaken. We start living as who we are—unlimited freedom, love and intelligence.

And that might look unlikely right now. There might be all sorts of protestations crowding into your mind about how real these issues are, how much responsibility you have, how you have to be realistic. I get that. I really do.

It is true that all these things limit our experience of freedom.

But not for the reasons we think they do.

Not because we need more or less of them to be free. (No matter how much that looks to be the case).

Precisely the opposite of this in fact.

They limit our experience of freedom because in that moment the thoughts of how restricted we are, of how impossible it is for us to flourish are absolutely compelling. They seem to be describing an objective, truthful reality.

But in that moment they are veiling the simple beingness of our true nature. They are veiling the fact that experience is ever-changing and has no truth in it. That we are only ever aware of being aware.

Nothing 'out there' and nothing 'in here' can limit our freedom because the only limit is a belief of things in relation to a belief of a self. And none of that is fixed, objective or true.

If you have, as you read through this book, even the slightest change of perspective on who you believe yourself to be and what you believe about the limits and obstacles in your life, it will be the tiny initial crack that breaks down the wall.

The realisation of your true freedom will eventually crash through and life will never be the same again.

LIFE WILL NEVER BE THE SAME AGAIN

THE BODY

If my body is enslaved, still my mind is free.
Sophocles

I was looking at the gunman's hand on my arm but I couldn't distinguish a physical end to my body and a start to his...
Mara Gleason, One Thought Changes Everything

We are all the same source. We are one, with no separation except for the illusion that we have our bodies.
Sydney Banks

Let's start with what looks, at least for me, most real, limiting and potentially restricting, with what seems to keep us fixed in time and place.

Our bodies.

You might already see this very differently. You might have experienced moments for yourself when it was clear that you are not limited by the boundaries, health, fitness, capacity, constraints and needs of the body.

You might already see that the body, no matter how it appears, is actually not separate from other bodies. That we are not the distinct, separate individual we believe ourselves to be. That the body itself is illusory.

You might have your own experience of being free regardless of apparent form. Maybe you have seen for yourself or in loved ones that ill health is no constraint on love and intelligence.

Maybe you have even seen that there is no end in death.

In which case you are helping the rest of us see it. You are helping me. Because even though I am writing this book on freedom, I still only rarely glimpse the freedom beyond apparent physical separation and constraints.

It seems that all we can ever do is to look towards what we know to be true and in doing that we come to what is really going on. And let's start with our understanding of how we experience the physical.

There is a video of a very young boy, maybe two or so, climbing up the steps to a slide, stopping every so often, getting to the top with a look of pure joy and then sliding down, big smile on his face.

Just like any other two year old with something to climb on and slide down, all over the world.

Except this little boy has no arms and no legs. He got himself to the top of the slide using his chin and the tiny finger and toe attached to his shoulder and hip. Each step of the slide was only slightly smaller than the length of his entire body.

We might watch him and we might see profound disability. Our mind might fill with horror at the restricted and difficult life that lies ahead of him. We may even, perhaps with an element of shame, feel shock at the sight of someone so different from us. Or pity. Or relief that it is not us or our children. Or amazement at the feats of which a human being is capable. We might feel inspired, uplifted, in awe. Or we might just see the every day unremarkable occurrence of a young boy climbing the stairs to a slide.

What he is thinking we don't know.

It is not in our control which thoughts come to mind and it is not in our control which of those thoughts are believed. But that is the only way we can experience his body.

Just as it is when we have any thought about our own body. When we look in the mirror and see ugliness or incapacity or beauty or health or illness or possibility.

Thought creates an experience of our body or another's. In other words WE EXPERIENCE THE PHYSICAL THROUGH THOUGHT.

It sounds such a simple line. But the implications for what this means for us and who we are in relation to an apparently fixed world of separate objects are enormous. Everything that is apparently physical - pain, pleasure, separation, no separation is experienced through the changing energy of thought.

The artist can experience the canvas as an unbearable restriction or as the frame which allows the imagination to soar. Or the frame, the brushes and artist's hands disappear in the pure conversion of formless to painted form. It is the same for us. Is an apparent physical constraint a limit or a launch pad or not even something? These are the glimpses and examples we have whether in ourselves or others of intelligence, love and freedom shining out.

Jean-Dominique Bauby, a former editor of French Elle, was paralysed by a stroke that left him unable to move any part of his body except blink his left eyelid. He wrote his masterpiece *The Diving Bell and the Butterfly* one letter at a time, blinking when his assistant, reading out the alphabet, said the letter required.

During the 27 years in which he was imprisoned, Nelson Mandela was bringing about the end of apartheid, ensuring his fellow inmates were being educated, supporting his family. Whatever the apparent physical constraints, his mind remained utterly free.

We experience ourselves through thought. We experience others through thought. Our idea of who we are lives in thought. Our idea of who other people are lives in thought. Beyond these ideas what is there? The space in which thought arises is awareness, is pure love.

It looks like when someone dies that they have gone. In reality they have not gone anywhere because the awareness and love that they really were is the same awareness and love that we are. The way we experienced them (through thought) while alive is still the same in death. As Byron Katie says, "No one can leave me."

My father was diagnosed with leukaemia when I was nine. Very quickly he started to get very ill. He became weaker and weaker and spent much time bedridden. Yet the love, intelligence and absent-minded genius of him was never limited. Life never, not for one second, stopped expressing itself through the sheer loving force of his presence.

And most of the time it looks to me that his life ended with his death. But then sometimes it comes to me that whether he is physically here or not, his life lives for me, as it always did, in the awareness that I make possible.

Thoughts can make a hell of his death or a heaven. They create the very real experience of grief or gratitude, desolation or hope. Those experiences are there to be lived. Our freedom lies in allowing it all, knowing we are space in which all it can take place. And that within this awareness that we are, it is impossible for us to lose anyone, impossible to be separate.

Mara Gleason, in the breath-taking introduction to her book 'One Thought Changes Everything,' describes being held at gun point by a man in Buenos Aires and the profound moment of clarity in which the realm of 'me' got out of the way. She says, '…for a moment, he and I were the same. I was in him and he was in me. We were one.'

And all of this points us lovingly and firmly to an idea that is way beyond our grasp other than in those moments when all thought of who we are is blown away.

That limits are never physical.

Separation is never actual.

Existence is never objective.

Who we really are is not separate from anything. Who we are is all of it and bodies and selves and circumstances and events (including all those apparent individuals mentioned in this chapter) appear and disappear within us.

We can never be limited and separated by a body that is made of transient thought. Even if most of the time, for some of us, that is impossible to comprehend.

FREE BEYOND FORM

THE WISH LIST

The only people for me are the mad ones, the ones who are mad to live, mad to talk, mad to be saved, desirous of everything at the same time, the ones who never yawn or say a commonplace thing, but burn, burn, burn like fabulous yellow roman candles exploding like spiders across the stars.

Jack Kerouac, On the Road

The music comes on and the three year olds start dancing. Jumping and twirling and laughing and bouncing and falling around. They can't help it. Because music is playing.

The entire experience of self, life and world is transient and ever-changing.

And this prompts the question: if we realise it is all so fluid why would we bother doing, creating or having anything?

Well, let's imagine my wish list was: to be a billionaire and super fit with abs and a beach house, perfect kids, great hair and a cupboard full of Green and Black's almond chocolate.

(Example randomly plucked out of thin air purely for illustration's sake. Obviously.)

Let's consider this wish list. Maybe it's a bit similar to yours. (If so we should share a house or at the very least a hairdresser). Or maybe you'd like a record contract. Or to play in the World Cup. Or to get into the jeans you wore ten years ago. Or to save the oceans. Or to write a best seller. Or to pay the rent. Or a partner who adores you. Or world peace. Or a private plane. Or a date with... Whatever. You get the idea.

There are two truths about that list and in those truths lie the secret to the heart's desire of every single individual on the planet.

The first truth is that every experience of anything on our wish list, whether we have it or not, is only ever thought believed in the moment. Essentially, the experience of having or not having is made up of thought momentarily fixed on as real and it will change.

What it means to have a billion pounds will change. What it means to be super fit will change. What it takes for me to see my children as perfect will change. What it means to have a house by the sea will change. Apart from great hair. Because what it means to have great hair won't... what? oh... you're right... that will change too...

It all changes and there is no limit to the shape and form that the experience takes. From moment to moment thoughts can create from any of it a goal, a burden, an asset, a source of pride or shame, a gift or a hassle, a reason to live, regret, desperation, a reason to be ashamed or proud, something to have at all costs, something that separates or connects me, something to escape from...

As a result of thoughts in any one moment I will feel happy, sad, anxious, relieved, calm, hassled, trapped…

It will look like these feelings are caused directly by what I have done, what I own, what is out there, what I have acquired, what I don't have but they never are.

So the second truth is that happiness, security, worth, who I am has zero to do with what I do, where I live, what I own, what is happening in the world, who I know. It is not even related to what my hair looks like (and yes that one has taken decades).

This means I can drop my entire wish list. I can see that life will not be better, I will not be permanently happy or fulfilled or not anxious as a result. And just to put the final full stop on this argument, I can also see that because it is all experienced in thought the definitive achieving of any of it is literally impossible. This is because all it takes is another thought along the lines of 'more / better / less / different needed' and we are plunged back into the needing and wanting.

And often what happens when we see this is that motivation, logically, falls through the floor. Well if it's not going to make me happy then what's the point? If it's not going to stop me worrying then why would I bother? If I don't need to prove myself, then… We stop. Everything we thought we were doing out of a need to validate ourselves or impress or create security or do what we thought was expected of us loses all value.

At this point we have a foundation of clarity. We are living closer to reality. We see the madness of trying to change a world made of thought in order that our thoughts be more peaceful. We realise that thoughts and feelings come and go, that we, as awareness of it all, are secure and fine exactly as we are.

And we could stay here in this peaceful soup of ours (nb not pea soup. That's a whole other thing). My dear friend and colleague Liz Scott described this as the warm bath. We know our thoughts create our reality so we can just stay here peaceful, warm, cozy, soft, in love with the world, not needing ever to do anything.

The noise of our thinking dissipates. Our mind becomes very very quiet.

And in that quiet, we can hear the eternal sound of life. It gently cups its hands around our ear and says…

'Why are you just sitting there?
Get up. Come on. There is stuff to do.'

Life is very direct you see. It knows how extraordinary it is. It knows that every detail, every colour and taste and texture, every mountain and valley appears and disappears. It knows there is nothing there and that this nothing is everything. It knows this is all one crazy dream and this gives it the lightness and ease of full expression. Life is hungry. It wants dessert before the main course. It is a dream kid in a dream fairground. It wants to explore and find out. It wants to play. It wants to see itself reflected in every rain shower, every water fall, every teardrop. It has things to say, stuff to do, countries and books and ideas to investigate. It is here to witness itself in conversation, laughter, passion, love. To admire its spectacular form in the full length mirror. This is its chance. Thanks to you, life has a body and senses and the marvellous, beguiling illusion of a separate self in a separate world. It is not going to pass up the chance.

It has no time for the nonsense of pretending you are somehow less than the extraordinarily magnificent life force that you really are. It can't be bothered with the illusion that you are separate from life living itself. It rolls its eyes at the idea that you are limited or vulnerable. Life can bring you into reality. In the full power of awareness and intelligence. Right now. There is stuff to do.

Some of these instructions from life are a no-brainer. We simply find ourselves drinking a glass of water or climbing into bed or waking up or saying the words or moving to a country that is perfect.

Some of it may just seem immediately like the coolest thing in the world. This is the 'hell yeah' that Steve Chandler describes. It is different for all of us. It comes with an 'obviously!' or a 'shit, who wouldn't?' A whole mind and body moving towards that which makes the simplest, most beautiful sense, knowing that none of it means anything.

Some of it though is an idea that directly challenges the beliefs we had thought we had seen through but hadn't. An idea to do a talk or write a paper or call someone might be terrifying. A whisper to apologise to a friend may challenge our pride so much as to seem impossible. A thought to travel beyond our comfort zone or exhibit our paintings or express our love for someone might shake us to the core. A prompt to take a stand for what we believe might seem dangerous.

Once life has spoken though, the only thing in its way is what we are thinking about ourselves or the world or other people at any one moment. And we've seen through all that remember? Remember that beautiful pea soup?

Understanding who we are, there is nothing that can ever prevent us doing what we are doing.

The music comes on and the three year olds start dancing. Jumping and twirling and laughing and bouncing and falling around. They can't help it. Because music is playing.

Aliveness is who you are and you are simply being invited to see that more clearly.

Say yes to life. Yes to being nothing but life. Yes to being.

It only has this one chance in that dream of the beautiful, able, miraculous body of yours, with those unique gifts of yours, that way of talking or listening or laughing or singing or writing or leading or creating or moving that only you have.

Its moment is here.

The music is playing….

FREE TO LIVE.

EMOTIONS

Waking up to your true nature, who you truly are, does not shield you from feelings and emotions. It actually has the opposite effect: open, vulnerable, real, sensitive, and raw. Pure and unconditional. Love.

Garret Kramer

When I get lonely these days, I think: So BE lonely, Liz. Learn your way around loneliness. Make a map of it. Sit with it, for once in your life. Welcome to the human experience.

Elizabeth Gilbert, Eat, Pray, Love

If you are like me, then the underlying reason for wanting more freedom may be the desire to be happier more of the time. It seems that eventually everything boils down to that. How can I only experience the positive emotions? How can I be happier?

The thing is, it is this search for permanent happiness or for a different mental state other than the one we are in that is one of the biggest obstacles between us and the experience of freedom.

We find the deep 'causeless joy' as Rupert Spira describes it, the true freedom at the centre of our being, when we see that avoiding sadness, insecurity and unease is utterly, absolutely, unarguably impossible. Unnecessary. Undesirable even.

The search for 'positive feelings and experiences' and avoiding 'negative' ones is what is keeping us stuck.

How can that be? Surely the whole point of life is to find what makes you happy and keep doing it? Isn't our purpose here on earth to enjoy being here on earth? Otherwise what . . . ? Why . . . ?

I totally bought into this. Clearly, the point of life was to be happy. I read hundreds of books and acted on thousands of adverts that told me so and told me how to be it. And if I wasn't happy, then obviously I had to change whatever it was that was taking away my God-given right to happiness. Happiness was a fixation, a goal, a birthright, a guiding principle, the emblem of success and a life-well lived. If someone asked how I was, I would say, "Fabulous. Really happy!" to show the world how well I was doing.

And I, believing this, along with everyone else who believes this, was in hell.

Because happiness is as out of our control as a butterfly landing on our finger. It is a fleeting feeling caused by a thought. Thoughts change all of the time. Some of the thoughts will be hung on to, believed and an experience will arise from that thought and if that is happiness, so be it. If it is not, then so be that as well.

In other words, happiness is random. It is ever changing. It is unpredictable. It is utterly unrelated to the outside world. It is here one moment, gone the next. It is only our birthright in as much as it is our birthright as a human to experience a myriad of human emotions: sadness, happiness, peace, irritation, frustration, joy, gloom, ecstasy. They are all there for us. All equally out of our control.

And until we see the truth of this, we are stuck believing that:

a) happiness is necessary

b) happiness depends on living the life and having the things that make us happy

When we believe this, and we experience not being happy, we panic. We think we have to fix it. We scrutinise our job, relationship, house, friends, family, car, income. Which of them is the culprit? And because we are looking at the world through the low energy of mind that caused the feeling of unhappiness in the first place, then all we see around us are problems to fix. Our job is too pressured/not challenging enough, our partner is too clingy/not interested, our house is too small/too big, our friends are demanding/disinterested, the income is too low and we are trapped/too high and we are trapped.

So we try to make the changes, we tinker around with all of this, trying to get back our happy. And our happiness will return, of course, because that is just the natural ebb and flow of the mind. And, of course, we believe that our changes have created that state.

"Excellent," we think, "life is exactly as I want it to be. I have the job, relationship, house, friends, family, car, income of my dreams."

But then . . . disaster! The energy of mind dips, and we get low, and again, we're not happy.

Now we have two options.

We can continue thinking there is something wrong with the life we're living, so we change the relatively new spouse for an even shinier one, for example, or move house or job for the eighth time.

Or we look around and think, "This is my dream life. And I'm still not happy. Therefore, there must be something wrong with *me*. Maybe it is my brain chemistry or my diet or my childhood or my personality." And we embark on either the fixing of ourselves, or we try and blank out the unhappiness through drink, drugs, sex, pills, shopping, food, work or whatever.

It is a highway to suffering. Because the entire search for happiness, the looking for it in possessions or relationships or the blaming of self when it proves elusive is based on a myth. It is based on the most powerful myth to have infiltrated society since sailors used multiple anchors to stop their ships sailing off the edge of the flat earth. (Thank you to Michael Neill for that awesome anecdote.)

All we need to know is that nothing we can do can make us unchangingly happy. Nothing will put permanent smiles on our faces. There will be moments of happiness and moments of sadness, moments of fear and moments of calm, moments of gasping insecurity and moments of peace, moments of high energy and moments of low—no matter what we own or where we live or what our parents did or whether we have children or what job we do or how much money we have or... or... or... or...

We can write out our wildest dreams on paper and go all out

to achieve them until all of us are there—eating Green and Black's, in our beach house, with our great hair, great abs and great piles of cash (Am I right…? No…? Really…?)—and there will still be moments when we are unhappy.

Happiness comes and goes. Energy ebbs and flows. We experience different feelings. This is perfect. That's the design. Not feeling happy is as natural and inevitable as clouds moving across the sun. That's all. Nothing to fix or change. Ever.

When we see this, then oh my god our lives open up. It is not just that the search for happiness is no longer taking up our time and energy, it is that in seeing its total irrelevance, we literally throw open the double doors of life.

When happiness is no longer a goal or a requirement, we are free to:

explore and experience

We were so vulnerable before. We had to have a guarantee that this country or this job or this relationship would make us happy before we could risk ourselves or the five remaining days of our holiday allowance.

Now that we see nothing can guarantee happiness—and, also, who cares?—then we are free to explore the world. We can hang out with the people who looked annoying before. We can go to places where the weather is wholly unpredictable. We can, just for the hell of it, take the job that, on paper, we are unsuited for. We can read the books and watch the programmes with which we disagree.

We can be in places and feel lonely. We can be out in the world and be rejected. We can say what we think and be labelled stupid. We can tell someone we love them, and they can look down at their feet and say nothing back.

It is all perfect. Because our goal is not to be happy (or accepted, confident, affirmed or secure). We are simply here to explore and experience the whole damn show.

listen and create

This transformed relationship with the outside world creates space for a transformed relationship with our inner world. We know that the outside world cannot guide our decisions, so we look inwards. We listen to what makes sense for us.

And this "what makes sense" is so much more stable, secure, honest, loving and insightful than our previous chasing of disappearing butterflies through a meadow.

From this place, we watch the energy of mind ebb and flow. We see the thoughts that come from this place and the feelings they create. We see how reality changes each moment, and we realise that we truly are the creative force of the universe. We act and we watch what emerges from that action, whether it is a simple phone call or a global empire.

And the beauty is . . . indeed, the freedom is . . . indeed, the miracle is that none of it, none of it, needs to make us happy.

FREE TO EXPERIENCE IT ALL

MONEY

All I have is all I need
and all I need is all I have in this moment.
Byron Katie

It would be logical to assume that a chapter on money in a book about freedom would be about how to earn enough to be free.

How to make sure you have so much money that you never have a thought of poverty or lack or homelessness again.

How you can relax in your penthouse, getting everyone else to do the daily grind, leaving you free as a bird.

Yes… ummm… sorry about that.

Because that's not even slightly what we will be talking about.

We won't be talking about it because freedom is 100% unrelated to money.

Again, cue the sound of readers who made it through the last annoying chapters now slamming the book shut or closing it down in disgust.

Because obviously money enables us to do things, increases our choices, sets us free.

Money is a real thing. It opens doors. Smooths life. Of course we need it to have freedom.

How does this 'freedom is unrelated to money' nonsense work with the fact that we have to spend our time doing stuff we don't want to do to pay for a roof over our heads and food for the table?

How does it work with the fact that I know I am poor? That I look around at other people and see what they can do, the places they can go, the opportunities they have? That I am trapped in a dead-end job? Freedom is only for those who have the resources to be free.

Well shall we take a look at what is really going on?

For sure, there are moments when we might feel sick with fear at how little we have, at how poor and vulnerable we are. We look at our bank balance and our income and what we owe and we panic. We look at the impossible choices and sacrifices it looks like we have to make. Our head fills with horror films of what will happen to us and our loved ones.

And there will be moments when we are so immersed in what we are doing that the idea of money, wealth or resources doesn't even cross our mind.

And there will be moments when we look around us and know without the slightest doubt that we have everything we need to do whatever we know to do. We know we are as free as a bird.

And there will be moments when we simply find ourselves

doing what we do and along the way we seem to provide for ourselves and our family.

There will be moments when there is no thought whatsoever of an I that is poor, of others that have more and of money that is limited or unavailable.

And the fascinating thing is that...

NONE OF THESE EXPERIENCES HAVE ANYTHING WHATSOEVER TO DO WITH HOW MUCH MONEY WE HAVE.

These experiences happen because thoughts about who we are and what we need and what we have to have to be OK appear and are believed and we feel the emotions that those thoughts create. Or they do not appear and we have no experience in that moment of a self that needs anything.

Experience of poverty or abundance comes and goes but that is not who we are. We are the space in which that experience appears and disappears. The awareness that we are is utterly unrelated to and unaffected by what we earn or what we own.

And our idea of who we are and what we need to be secure, when it sees the truth of this, can settle in to that. It can disappear in the simple doing and being and knowing. It can disappear in the knowledge that a restricted, limited past, present or future is only ever a trick of a mind designed to turn us into a restricted, limited, apparently real self.

For this idea of who we are to survive it has to fight and resist and suffer. It has to deny the truth of perfection right now. It has to make out that there is something missing or that something has to be resisted. Because that is the only way it can exist.

Louis CK, the comedian, tells a story of being on a plane the first time they were trialling on-board wifi. He said that the steward announced with a fanfare that the wifi was on and everyone took out their phones to try it out.

The passengers were all trying to get into the internet and it turned out not to be working. 'Oh for f**ks sake' said the man in the seat next to Louis, rolling his eyes in irritation.

Louis said he looked at the man thinking, "You are on a chair. In the middle of the sky. Flying thousands of miles an hour. And you are pissed off because something that didn't exist until 2 seconds ago isn't available to you right now.... Why are you not just here speechless in awe?"

Great question. And the only reason we are not constantly living from this state of awe, not constantly gazing with wide open eyes at the sheer crazy miraculous abundance of life all around us is because sometimes thoughts are believed of how this moment or this experience should be different in some way.

A thought appears of an idea of 'I' and another thought appears that the 'I' needs more money. It looks like the picture of us in a sleeping bag on the pavement is really who we are. It looks as though those images of us making the wrong choices in the past are really who we are. It looks like we are a failure. It looks as though there are things we want to do but can't because we can't afford to. It looks like other people are better off than us. It looks like money is limiting our potential.

And this has nothing to do with money. Nothing. And nothing to do with who really are.

It has everything to do with the creative power of thought to create a world of restriction and limits. A limited, fearful, insecure self that will only be OK once certain conditions are met.

And when we truly see thoughts for what they are then made up comparisons to a rosier future, better-off people or more desirable circumstances fall away and we are just here right now, seeing with clear eyes, listening with true ears, doing what we are doing and experiencing the miracle of this with every cell of our bodies.

In these moments of absolute clarity, we go beyond appreciation, beyond gratitude to some other place where we are everything, we have everything. As Tony Parsons describes it, we are 'being bombarded by love through the senses, through everything that is.' The entire universe and everything in it is ours because it only exists through us. It only exists for us.

To say we experience wealth in these moments is the ultimate understatement.

In those moments when we know we are the wealth and pure luxury of life itself, we know that any experience of poverty is just the appearance of a thought-created poor I. We can know this whether we are sitting on a throne or on the pavement.

We can also realise that there is no amount of money that can block the thought 'I need more'. There is no amount of funds saved or earned that can make the belief 'I could lose everything' or 'I am vulnerable' less believable. We know that these thoughts can appear whether we are in the marble lobby of our Swiss bank or pushing a trolley containing all our worldly possessions.

The drive to earn money in order to be secure comes from a

belief in an 'I' that believes it needs to earn a certain amount to safeguard a non-existent future.

This is a drive that will never be fulfilled.

As long as the thought of a needy I is believed, we can never earn or save enough. All that it takes is a new thought 'need more to be OK' and we are straight back into the experience of poverty.

Believing ourselves somehow separate from creation, we believe that 'richness' has to be created. We think we have to force the conditions in ourselves or the world to make money.

We talk about money with clients with a glaringly fake nonchalance. We hover over every penny, every apparent unfairness. We suspect the world of cheating us. Our grip is tight because our entire sense of self depends on it.

Or we hide away from it. Freezing like a rabbit in the headlights anytime it is mentioned. Unable to discuss or enquire or consider options and possibilities.

Thoughts about scarcity and limit create a reality of scarcity and limit. It cannot work any other way.

What is interesting is that, as we take this idea of a thought-created vulnerable 'I' and its thought-created needs less seriously, motivation changes.

As these thoughts become less believable we start seeing the dream of this. Motivation driven by insecurity and lack of worth falls away.

And the fascinating question is what happens when the illusion is revealed for what it is? What is heard when we aren't listening to the noise of our insecure thinking and our terror about what money means?

We hear the whisper of who we really are. We hear love and freedom. We hear inspiration. We hear life. And we go along with this whisper, we go along with what we find ourselves doing because there isn't a single reason not to.

The experience and knowledge of being abundant, extravagant wealth, right now, exactly as we are, frees us up to see that we are just doing what we are doing. All from this place of knowing we are all of it.

From the obvious abundance and the breath-taking certainty, clear, simple reality becomes visible.

Now we are coming from the inside 100%. We have dropped all the horror stories we used to have about money and the future. Now we are listening in to what is going on on the inside and we watch what is being done.

All of it comes with a settled, natural feeling of this makes sense to do, offer, write, put out there, ask for, find out, explore. And the world responds accordingly of course, because it is our world created in consciousness. Knowing that it is our world, we act, speak, explain, ask, suggest and question from absolute integrity. And the thought-created people of our world say yes or no and we know it is perfect either way.

Now, seeing that everything we perceive is who we are, we are rich beyond our wildest dreams and the world is our playground. We are sitting on a beach that stretches as far as the eye can see creating sand castles out of the perfectly mouldable sand. We are an artist with as many canvases and paints as we desire. We are planting in paradise with access to the ultimate on-line garden catalogue.

We realise that the world is a treasure trove full of sensory greatness to experience and that's what we're here for.

And through this realisation we move through this world in total freedom, without a penny to our name.

Or we move through the world in total freedom, creating and distributing billions of dollars in every waking moment.

Or anything in-between. Who cares which? Or changing all the time. Who cares?

What is seen in form will make so much sense, will be so obvious that it will be the natural, integral, inevitable expression of the love and freedom of life. It will have no meaning or significance. There will be no idea of success or failure. It will just be the simplicity of being appearing in an apparent world. The reflection of a mind so at home in itself that it has merged into life and love and can only see life and love.

We are the richness of each moment, of infinite potential, of unbounded awareness.

Anything less than that is a misunderstanding.

FREE TO EXPERIENCE WEALTH

THE SYSTEM

When I walked out of prison, that was my mission, to liberate the oppressed and the oppressor both.
Nelson Mandela

Lighthouses don't go running all over an island looking for boats to save; they just stand there shining.
Anne Lamott

Peace doesn't require two people. It requires only one. It has to be you. The problem begins and ends there.
Byron Katie

How does this understanding work when the whole system is corrupt? When it seems impossible to be free because the system is stacked against us?

In those moments, we experience a them and us. There are victims and villains. We feel trapped and stuck. It looks impossible that anything can change.

Hopeless and despairing are not our nature. That is not who

we are. That's why it feels so off. We can use these feelings as a sign to look deeper into what is going on.

They tell us that we are missing something. They tell us that we are not seeing clearly who we are and what the world is. Stuck and trapped and believing thoughts that tell us life is impossible, we are in no position to change the world.

Because the world only exists in the way it does in that moment because of thought believed.

Seeing this more clearly changes everything – everything we believe about ourselves, what we want, who we are, the world we live in.

And one of the things that turns upside down is how we understand integrity.

If we look at the word and its Latin root integritas, we see that originally it meant soundness, wholeness or completeness.

What is soundness, wholeness or completeness for a human being? It is the knowledge that we are everything, that we are everything we perceive and everything we perceive is who we are. The idea of self, other people, circumstances, events, nature emerges through us moment by moment.

Violence. Harassment. Secretism. Racism. Greed. Agism. Infidelity. Slander. Sexism. Nepotism. Jealousy. Lying. Killing. Stealing. Privilege. Fraud.

The boundaries, meanings and implications slip and slide over each other. How we class and define where any of this begins and ends, exists or not. How we judge. Where we draw lines. What we accept and reject. What we forgive and what causes life-long hostility. What is grounds for mass protest or what is accepted without challenge. What is rewarded by society, what is condemned. What is accepted in law, what is punishable by death. All of it is arbitrary, transient. Decided by the ebb and flow of thought and the arbitrariness of belief alone.

When we stand up for what we think and believe we are standing up for a stream of thoughts that varies according to whatever state of mind we are in, as an individual, group, nation or planet, at any one time.

It makes no sense to react against this transient reality, to believe we have moral superiority over it. But of course that is what most of us spend most of our time doing. Because we have this idea that we are a separate self and that separate self can only define itself by separation.

This is the origin of every argument, every act of terrorism whether taking place in the kitchen or across the planet.

As we look in the direction of what is real, of what is actually happening in our minds, we own this projection.

We can't be responsible for it because we don't control which thoughts come to mind but we can own it. We can only honour the truth that somehow this reality is created within awareness. We realise we are the custodian of this projection. There is no them, there is no right or wrong, there is only creation in thought and awareness of that creation.

Now what? What difference does that make?

It creates an enormous shift that transforms the rest of our lives. That's what.

It means that instead of exhausting ourselves fighting illusory enemies, we get clear as to their nature. We come from love and we see that they are us. People who believe their thoughts. Just us believing our thoughts of separation, reflected back.

We start to realise that the bad stuff will only leave the world when we stop perpetuating it. There is nothing to stand against, there is only thoughts and beliefs to see more clearly. We get real with ourselves.

I want the end of harassment? Well then who in this dream world am I harassing?

I want the end of sexism, racism or agism? It begins with the dissolving of every thought about separation and superiority that I have ever believed.

I want the end of violence? How am I violent in thought, feeling or action?

I want to stand for love? Do I love every hater? Do I realise I am every hater? No? Then let's start there.

Until I can show how it is done, how what I want is even possible, I can't expect it from anyone else.

When I move beyond conditioned fears and insecurities, I see that there is no one else anyway.

It begins and ends with me. I am all of it. Integral. Whole. Complete. Entire.

FREE TO CHANGE THE WORLD

OTHER PEOPLE

When you think everything is someone else's fault, you will suffer a lot. When you realise that everything springs only from yourself, you will learn both peace and joy.
Dalai Lama

Unarmed truth and unconditional love will have the final word in reality
Martin Luther King

Other people get in the way. They slow us down. They cause fear and anger. They create pain. They have demands. They challenge us emotionally. They sap our energy. They overload and over-stretch us. We have to look after them or worry about them. They restrict us and limit us.

In a typical week in my coaching practice, on social media, in the headlines, in opinion polls, in agony columns, in my own life and family, this is confirmed over and over again.

Whether it is parents worrying over their child's behaviour.

Or adult children needing to put time and money into helping their ageing parents. Walking on egg shells around a volatile partner. The agony of watching the suffering of others on the news. Or the terror of racism. The hell of sexual harassment or bullying. Or road rage. Or men in general. Or women in general. Or Trump. Or the neighbours. Or the mother in-law. Or the slimy colleague making us look bad. Or the slow person at the front of a queue when we have a train to catch.

It seems the world is full of people who, intentionally or not, knowingly or obliviously, affect our happiness and security, who limit our lives, who get in the way of our freedom.

We do everything we can to create a life given the restrictions that other people create. We need to make sure the people we love are happy so that we can be happy. We need to make sure the people we rely on don't change their minds so we can be secure. We need to make sure the people who frighten us with their beliefs, behaviour or power are made to change. This can be exhausting. No wonder we don't have time to do the stuff we really want to do. No wonder we feel trapped.

Or we live in the equivalent of a cave. Withdrawing into a smaller world. Shunning the individuals or groups who cause us fear or anger. Not risking relationships in case we are betrayed. Pulling up the drawbridge because individuals or groups of people are so toxic or dangerous. Yet no matter what we do, they are always out there. Haunting our thoughts and our dreams. No wonder we don't feel free to live life.

Hmmm. Where do we go with this? I for one don't want to spend the rest of my life tormented and held back by the emotions and actions of other people. Not much freedom in that.

Well how about we look a bit more carefully at this whole set up? How about we consider that we are living a belief that is actually not true.

How about we consider the fact that no one has the power to make us happy, sad, scared, secure, insecure, traumatised, lonely, desperate?

Ever.

Let's look at this crazy idea in relation to the quality that causes us to feel what other people feel, that seems to be the reason why the suffering of others limits our emotional freedom – empathy.

And let's look at it in relation to the protective device deemed necessary in any relationship – boundaries.

Empathy

Empathy is seen as one of the most fundamental qualities of human kind. Our ability to know and feel another person's experience is indicative of an evolved and emotionally intelligent person.

What a wonderful idea.

What a shame it is an utter illusion.

I see my child distraught, crying and I am devastated. I feel her sadness. I myself am immersed in whatever emotion is swamping her body. I feel so distraught myself, I fully know what she must be feeling.

Except I don't.

How can I?

How can I possibly ever have any idea of what it feels like to be her at any moment ever. I don't know what is going on in her body or mind. I don't know what sensations she is experiencing. I never will. Even if she tells me, I still have no idea what personal, momentary experience she is trying to convey. I can only experience my imagination of her sadness. I never have any idea of another's experience.

'OK', you might say. *'I concede that. But you can see her crying. You can see how sad she is. And that is making you sad. It is only natural and expected for you to be sad when your daughter is sad.'*

Well, not only do I have absolutely no idea what experience she is having at that moment, my sadness is not caused by hers in anyway.

If it were, everyone seeing her tears or cries would have the same response. They don't.

If it were, every time she cried I would have the same response. I don't.

Another's experience or emotional state can never cause an emotional state in me.

This is because my entire experience comes from thought in the moment not from anything that I see around me.

And it is true in every single case.

Every time a post about violence makes me feel sick and shaky with how much I empathise with the victim, I am in a dream. It is not their pain I am experiencing. It is an experience of pain generated through what is momentarily believed. Absolutely nothing to do with the experience of anyone else.

Every time I see news reports of a boat load of refugees or a camp of starving children or people sitting in bomb torn homes and I feel their absolute desolation, I am in a dream. It is not their deprivation and hardship I am experiencing. The feelings of sadness and helplessness come from what is believed. They are not the sadness and helplessness of another. They are not caused by any image, any situation, any people. They are caused by thought believed in that moment.

In other words thought believed in a given moment can create an idea of others , an idea of others suffering and an idea of a self (me) that should be doing something about it.

Great. (Said with sarcasm.) *So what is the outcome of this? If we take away the belief in empathy and in the objective existence of others will we lose our fundamental humanity? Will we become psychopaths? Cold hearted callous bastards and bitches ignoring others in pain because it is 'all just an illusion'. How will I know who to help and what to do? How will I connect with people and show I care about them? How will I fix issues in my kids, my colleagues, the world?*

We'll get there. But first let us consider boundaries…

Boundaries

We all know boundaries are important and necessary, right? We have to set them for our children so that they know what behaviour we won't tolerate, so they grow into responsible adults that respect other people. We have to set them at work so we don't get dumped on. We have to set them with other people so we don't get taken advantage of. We have to set them with our partner so that they don't have affairs all over the place and leave the top off the toothpaste.

Boundaries are about self protection, self-esteem, self-confidence and self respect. They are necessary in a society in which different interests conflict. It looks like establishing boundaries helps us carve out more freedom for ourselves.

What a wonderful idea.

What a shame, it is an utter illusion.

Boundaries, like empathy, are one of the wonderful creations of a self that believes it is separate from what it perceives.

Let's look at what is really going on.

The fact is that I cannot experience anyone else, not even those closest to me, other than through thought in the moment. I cannot experience my partner or my boss or my colleagues directly. I cannot even experience my idea of who I am without thought.

Experience of all of these people – colleagues, children, neighbours, bosses, even ourselves – is created from moment to moment, appearing and disappearing, brought to life in the temporary experience that thought creates and then shapeshifting into something else or dissolving altogether.

Another way to look at it is that I am all of it. I am the whole experience. There is no outside world in the way my mind creates it. There are no other objective, independent people with personalities and the power to affect me no matter what it looks like. There is no permanent self with fixed characteristics that has to be protected, no matter how much that seems to be the case.

There is just the energy of thought creating one experience after another of an outside world, of other people, of a self called Clare. And boundaries themselves are part of this illusion.

I cannot build a moat around a castle that is made of thin air.

I cannot put armour on a self that morphs from one moment to the next. I cannot shield myself from others because as long as I am believing that others cause me to suffer they always will. The moat, the armour, the shield, the boundaries are as made of thought and are as subject to constant change as the self they are deemed to protect and the other people they are deemed to keep away.

Great. (Again, said with sarcasm. Perhaps even more than before.)

So what is the outcome of this? If I drop the belief that boundaries are necessary will I turn into a total doormat, gasping 'do what you want' as the crowd stampedes over me. Will I put myself in danger? Will I open myself up to people who will steal from me, violate me, laugh at me, disrespect me? How do I navigate a world that changes from moment to moment according to my state of mind?

Let's see.

***

There is no possibility of empathy in a world in which an emotional reaction to what another is feeling or experience is created by thought believed in that moment and not by what another is going through.

There is no possibility that boundaries are anything other than changing thought in a world which is simply our moment to moment experience of thought reflected out.

The marvel of this realisation is that it takes us into reality. (That is what realisations do after all). We come as close as it is humanly (i.e. with a human body that apparently ties us into the world of form) possible to get to what is actually happening.

What is actually happening is that sometimes we have the

gift of an experience that looks like it is caused by something outside us. We get to see an objective world of self, of other people, of situations, of bosses. We are conscious of this experience as though it is real, as though its existence has nothing to do with the awareness that we make possible.

This same gift – consciousness – also enables us to see that this whole incredible special effects, high definition film we are experiencing is *only* possible because of the awareness that we are somehow bringing about.

We start to notice how the hell of other people is really the heaven. The heaven of being given a body and a human experience and senses and feelings and a rollercoaster ride from joy to distress, love to hate. This is what people queue for hours for in Disney Land. This is being alive.

Without that separation, without the illusion of other people, there would be no experience of self. We would not have the ability to realise that consciousness creates and allows an experience of others as if it were really coming from them.

Empathy and boundaries are part of this gift. In the moments when it looks as though our sadness is caused by the sadness of another or that our separation is necessary (or even possible) we are in the experience. There is nothing we can do but live it. That is the gift of it.

And sometimes we look into the eyes of another and we see the miracle. We see the perfection of that other and we see that perfection made possible in consciousness. We see that we are all of it. The magnificence of whatever we are is reflected back, we see the other and ourselves as who we really are.

There is stillness. There is absolute peace. There is the dissolving of assumptions and the fading of projection.

Nothing has to change, not even our suffering. There is just the one all-encompassing experience. There is doing or not doing. In the space we say anything, ask for anything knowing whatever the response is, it is perfect. Knowing we are only asking ourselves. For the briefest of moments, there is absolute love, absolute freedom.

And then it shifts again and we are straight back into the illusion. Hair streaming back, eyes wide as the roller coaster accelerates, rockets, plunges into the heaven and hell of the joy, calm, terror, love, dependency, excitement and limits of an apparently real, apparently separate world. The whole rainbow. The fragile, ever-changing, infinite combinations of the kaleidoscope of a made up reality. For as long as we are in it, our hearts seem to be, to use that wonderful expression, walking around outside our body. We feel vulnerable. We feel limited by and dependent on others. It looks like we have to control and change others in order to be OK, in order to be free.

And then we stop. We realise. We see that we are all of it. That our freedom can never be limited by another because that other is only ever who we are.

Separation is the gift of human life. Without separation, we would never know that there is nothing to separate.

The illusion of constraints and pain created by other people helps us to see that we are truly free. Without it we would never experience freedom. We would never experience the pure love of who we are.

FREE TO BE LOVE

YOUR THING

You are not controlling the storm,
and you are not lost in it. You are the storm.
Sam Harris, Free Will

What's your Thing?

No, not the thing that everyone knows you love. The 80s disco music or classic cars or siamese cats or sudoko or golf.

No, I mean the Thing. The Thing that makes you go a bit doolally. You know that Thing?

The Thing that instantly makes you tense up, that you need to hyper control, that gives you sleepless nights with your mind whirring around every angle?

Or the thing that is so scary you can't even look at it directly? That you can't talk about. The thing that is so worrying you pretend that you couldn't care less about it. Looking off to one side while it looms larger and larger in the corner of your vision.

Yeah. That Thing.

A client was telling me about his wife tightly managing everything in their lives—their finances, food, clothes, holidays. He said, "She's so controlling about everything that it makes me stressed, and then I just want to just forget about it all and let her get on with it. Who cares anyway?"

Control or giving up?

Micro-management or escapism?

There is something that looks like it causes a problem, and we either grit our teeth through the stress of pinning down every detail or we give up altogether. The mental leap between "all over it" and "having none of it."

Teenagers who are up all night studying or who pretend illness because they are anxious about a bad mark.

Business clients who stress over every word or who abandon a programme before its even launched because they are worried no one will sign up.

Strict dieters being hyper vigilant about every calorie and then eating junk for days after they have broken one of their food rules.

All or nothing.

To explore this further, and because I am a down-with-the-kids, modern sort of coach (really I am), I'm calling these two ways of being:

wev—which is short for *whatev*, which is short for *whatever*, which is short for *Talking about this is doing my head in; do whatever you want!* (with optional 'W' hand shape); and

sfs—an acronym for "so f*****g stressed!"

They look like they are on opposite sides:

wev, with its dismissive "who cares, anyway?' checking out, hands over our ears "la la la" and blank disengagement.

sfs, with its tightness, control, anxiety and perfectionism.

Yet, they both come from the same place.

A belief in the power of an idea of a thing to make an idea of a self feel something.

With wev, the thing looks so complicated, important or scary that we feel hopeless to approach it in any way. Even conversations about it make us so uncomfortable that we have to close them down. Separation of self from Thing is the only option.

With sfs, the thing looks so big, complicated, important or scary that we have to climb all over it, choke the air out of it. Disagreement, risk or deviation from the plan cannot be tolerated. Tight control by self of Thing is the only option.

wev and sfs may take our behaviour in different directions, but both are based on the same illusion: that this Thing and any inability to master it says something about us.

Whether it is money, a diet, a programme, a conversation, an exam, an idea, a life . . . there is so much freedom in seeing that this "Thing," no matter how real it looks, is an experience created in thought and brought alive in awareness as if it were objective and categorical.

There is so much freedom in seeing that *nothing* is objectively real in the way we believe it to be, *nothing* says anything about us, *nothing* means success or failure. It is impossible for us to accurately and consistently define ourself in relation to something created from thought. The reality of the Thing only exists in the way it is believed to exist, right now, and that will change.

When we realize this, wev and sfs dissolve into thin air. Stressing about an illustrated story will seem a bit effortful. Running away from a painted monster will seem a bit over the top.

In this way, no longer living a story, we hang out in reality. In reality, we get to live in a state of simple curiosity, in open awareness. We have conversations with people. We find out stuff. We ask. We listen. We suggest things.

No matter what has gone before, no matter how dire things look, there is always the possibility of a whole new understanding of who we are and of what is real, a whole new perspective that will open doors and windows for a fresh spring breeze.

When we come into the simplest possible reality, we notice the light switches we had missed before as we frantically crashed around in the darkness or when we took ourselves out of the room altogether.

With none of it meaning anything, we find ourselves engaging with the people, the ideas, the life that are right there in front of us and that aren't there at all.

This is real dream living. Living in reality with the wev and the sfs a distant memory. Living infinite creative potential.

FREE TO ENGAGE

RESPONSIBILITY

In the highest place you are attached to nothing.
You are neither attached not detached you are beyond all qualification, beyond all quality.
You are the informationless being.
Mooji

Responsibility doesn't exist. It seems like we are responsible but knowing who we truly are beyond the concepts of an identity allows us to navigate this experience with love , clarity and understanding.
Responsibility takes care of itself.
Grayson Hart

So this is a book about the myth of objective reality. About how all experience is thought brought alive in consciousness. How nothing we perceive is as we perceive it.

The slight problem with this is that it looks like total b******t.

Because obviously things are real.

There are tax returns to complete and bills to pay and meetings to attend and customers to serve and washing up to do and forms to fill in and rubbish to put out. There is a load of responsibility on our shoulders.

To say this is not real is nonsense.

Let's take a responsibility that some of us have to deal with - putting the rubbish out.

Tomorrow the bin men will come. If the bins don't get put out on the street this evening, they won't get emptied. If they don't get emptied there won't be space for any more rubbish.

Bins. Binmen. Rubbish to be taken out.

Reality. Responsibility. And no freedom.

So how does that work with the understanding that all experience is created in thought?

If I stare long enough at the rubbish while contemplating consciousness will it disappear in a beam of light?

If I meditate on the nature of thought will the bins walk themselves out to the street outside?

Hasn't worked so far. Not even when I turn on my Himalayan salt lamp. Nothing. Not one inch do those bins move.

They are real and solid, they exist, they are in my life.

And yet…

And yet I can see that it is perception that gives these bins reality and meaning.

In the experience of say an eight year old goat-herd in the

remotest tribe, these bins, indeed bins and bin men in general quite possibly have no reality whatsoever.

If I gathered together all the people in the world (including all the bin men and goat-herds) and brought them to stand directly in front of the bin and said 'look at this' there would be 7 billion experiences of reality in that moment which may or may not include bins.

Not one of those experiences would match mine.

Not one of those experiences would be more right or more real than mine.

Each would appear 100% real, 100% right.

As experience changes, bins exist or don't exist, are relevant or irrelevant, ugly or useful or dirty or smelly or clean or overfull. Taking them out can seem a burden or easy or something I do while chatting on the phone to my mum without even noticing. They can be the reason to be annoyed (in those retro-moments when I do secretly, don't tell my Mum, believe it is a job for a man). They can seem like a symbol of a shockingly wasteful society or of a highly organised civilised system.

An idea of bins comes and goes. The definition and meaning they have in their moments of existence slips and slides. All according to perception in the moment. The bins exist because perception allows them to exist.

It is exactly the same with this self that seems to be me. Hundreds, maybe even thousands of versions of it. None of them (not even mine) more right or real than another.

So this leaves us in a predicament.

It gives us an understanding of the shifting, sliding nature of reality and at the same time we still live in an apparently real world of kids to feed, washing up to do, tax returns to fill in, and bins to take out to the street.

So now what?

We look at what connects the two.

We look at the bridge between the understanding of how experience is created and the experience itself.

This bridge is the space in which experience is created. It is the apparent perceiver of the experience.

This is the idea and the experience of the self, the personal, the 'I'.

As long as there is an 'I, Clare' that believes it is a fixed, objective real self there will be a world of objects, people, events and circumstances that also look fixed, real and objective. These will appear harmful or pleasurable or annoying or helpful to me. I will seek to change the world or myself in order to feel secure and happy.

As long as there is an identification of self with consciousness, it will look like my experience has something to do with me. As long as it looks like objects appear in 'my' awareness, I will seek to change my thoughts or my perspective to feel secure and happy. There will be responsibility and there will be a feeling of not being free.

As this identification with made up self or separate consciousness wanes, everything changes.

The 'I' and the 'me' and the 'mine' see through themselves. Consciousness rises to such an extent that it is clear there is no 'I' to protect, there is no 'me' to change things and there is no 'I' that can be aware.

This can last a moment before the 'I' looks rock solidly real again or it can last a life time. It doesn't matter either way. The illusory 'I' gives all the roller coaster thrills of the illusory world. It gives the drama of apparent choice and control. The tension of imagined risk and failure.

The state of no 'I' gives the gift of being, the gift of aliveness in which security, safety and well-being are such a given that they don't even exist as concepts.

In those moments when the 'I' dissolves, there is marvel, there is pure love, there is wholeness. There is doing because it would be impossible not to do. There is no concern as to outcome. There is no desire to feel differently. There is simple movement, simple action, natural, unstoppable and inevitable.

The washing up is done. The tax return is filed.

The bins are taken out.

And as to who or what is taking the bins out?

Maybe we'll find out one day.

For now, it's enough to know: it's not us.

FREE TO LET RESPONSIBILITY TAKE CARE OF ITSELF

SELF-IMPROVEMENT

The most fundamental aggression to ourselves, the most fundamental harm we can do to ourselves, is to remain ignorant by not having the courage and the respect to look at ourselves honestly and gently.

Pema Chödrön

I spent decades believing that I had to improve and develop myself in order to fulfil my potential. According to where I was working, who I was admiring, what I was watching or reading, how I was being told to be, I knew I had to be stronger, cleverer, wittier, funnier, fitter, better dressed, more ambitious, beautiful, creative, decisive, organized, articulate, charismatic and on and on . . . Only then would I be able to fully live. Only then would I be free.

There was no end of flaws to correct and a deluge of self-help books, self-development courses, and self-denigration to the point of self-obsession followed.

And then I came across this understanding of the nature of our experience that has put an end to all of that. It describes how experience of self, life, other people, and the world is a transient creation of thought. The more aware we are of the creative power of thought the more arbitrary and momentary we realise our actual 'reality' to be.

Through this understanding, we come to realise that, like any other thoughts, a "flaw" or "imperfection" perceived in ourselves or someone else is simply a belief in that moment. And that the opinion changes from person to person, moment to moment, mind-state to mind-state. Porridge can be too hot, too cold or just right or not noticed, not eaten, irrelevant, and all of those judgements depend on whether it is Goldilocks eating it or someone else and what Goldilocks believes about porridge.

If we think we have flaws—in appearance, character, ability, mentality—then we can set out, as I did, on a lifetime trying to correct them, and the multibillion-dollar self-improvement industry gets a new recruit. Or, we can set out on a lifetime of pretending "self-acceptance." ie. I have this flaw, but I'm pretending to myself that it doesn't exist. And none of it works, because the more we try to accept or correct these "flaws," the more real we think they are. The more real we think they are, the more we think we have to do something about them, and the more real they seem.

Let's not underestimate the power of this vicious circle of believing critical thoughts. People can believe themselves so flawed that they act on the thought that the world would be better without them. Or we can believe our security to be so threatened by other people that they deserve disrespect, ill-treatment or even to be killed. A world of violence to self or others can disappear the minute we realize the nature of it.

If everything we think about ourselves and others is simply a thought that can change, then we are left with the enormous question: Who are we?

In the truest possible sense, we are nothing. We are not a fixed entity in any way. We are presence that experiences and lives a life according to thought at that moment. There is nothing that cannot change from one thought to another. No fixed self, no fixed personality or identity, no fixed character, no flaws, no imperfections. In our clearest understanding, we are witness to the beliefs and thoughts about all those things. We are never those things.

And while we are nothing, we are also everything. Everything we experience about the world, ourselves and other people is in the awareness that we somehow make possible. This room, this sky, those people, that tree, this feeling. None of this would exist without us. We are everything.

Nothing and everything.

Impossible even to define.

FREE TO BE

IDENTITY

I'm not in control, it's not all on me, and I am free to have my experience because it's happening. All the struggle, pain and illusion are perfect.
Every waking up is perfect.
Amanda Jones, Uncovery

I was watching the school swimming gala. Some of the kids were like little dolphins gracefully and powerfully making their way down the pool. Others put forth the most tremendous amount of effort, legs and arms flailing and fitfully made it, exhausted and panting, to the edge. Some sat on the side in their uniforms, not wanting to swim.

I was watching all this going on and started thinking about how I and my clients, and pretty much everyone I know, have lives like this. Some aspects of life are straightforward, some seem to take tremendous effort, and some are not even attempted.

And looking at the pool and the kids doing whatever they

were doing, I realized that it just doesn't matter. The dolphins were flashing through the water, the strugglers received huge cheers at the finish, those sitting it out were just sitting it out. It really didn't matter either way.

Because the truth is that all of us were under the same leisure centre roof for that hour, supported by the same planet. Sitting, standing or in the water; watching, cheering or swimming, we were all of us just having an experience of life in that moment.

Winning or losing, effortful or effortless, full in or full out, it just didn't matter. It doesn't matter, ultimately, because the only thing that makes it anything other than the simple, miraculous experience of life is thought in the moment, and this will change.

This is the truth of every single experience we have. It is true of winning or losing, taking part or sitting out. It is true of life itself, and it is true of all the areas of life we get to experience—career, marriage, finances, sport, kids, friends, family, health, swimming . . .

And this, my friends, is where life gets interesting, weird, logical and annoyingly/delightfully paradoxical.

Allow me to explain.

When we see that any experience is just an experience, we have the mind-blowing realization that we don't need to try to excel in it, change it, struggle in it or avoid it in order to feel OK.

We are perfectly OK regardless.

We are just in the leisure centre of life, totally fine. (That analogy only works if you like leisure centres. Many don't. In fact I don't even like them that much. Feel free to substitute for something else.)

As we realize that everything we think about an experience—or about ourselves having an experience—is simply thought in the moment, then any idea we have about the experience or about ourselves having that experience loses its grip. Identity and necessity become less compelling.

No longer believing that we cannot swim (or do anything else), we are free to give swimming (or anything else we are moved to do) a go. We can mess up, we can look goofy, we can splash around, we can do whatever occurs to us, and we can have fun with it all.

As we drop any idea of swimming being hard work or drop the need to struggle, we relax, we draw on the simple movements, remember what we know, we take out the effort and exhaustion, energy is freed up, flows.

As we realize that coming in first, second, third or last has no bearing whatsoever on who we are and what we are capable of, we are free to simply experience the race.

This is the win-win-win of life.

This is the exit from all those crazy catch-22s that self consciousness sets up such as:

'In order for me to see myself as a swimmer, I have to swim. I can't swim until I see myself as a swimmer.'

'In order for me to be a good swimmer, I have to relax in the water. I can't relax until I am a good swimmer.'

'In order for me to be a great swimmer, I have to win this race. I won't win this race until I know I am a great swimmer.'

The irony, paradox, annoying/delightful secret to life is that when we are open to the whole thing— swimming/not swimming, struggling/not struggling, winning/not winning —we are free.

We can substitute anything for *swimming* here—writing, making friends, cycling, doing a sport, growing a business, passing exams, managing a project, getting fit, eating alone, being a parent, speaking in public, climbing a mountain, visiting a new country, taking a stand, painting a picture, running for office . . . anything.

When we are open to whatever there is to experience, our experience of life, of ourselves, of what we can do and create blows the roof off the leisure centre.

When we realise that our identity as "champion swimmer," "struggling swimmer," or "non-swimmer" has no truth or relevance, we realise we are simply experiencing being in the water or not in the water, doing whatever occurs to us to do in the moment.

And the crazy, amazing thing is that whether we see this or not, it just doesn't matter.

Because, either way, we're all just free to be here in the leisure centre together. Free to experience life. Free to do whatever makes sense to us.

FREE TO SWIM. FREE TO DO ANYTHING

PROBLEMS

Reality is only a Rorschach ink-blot, you know.
Alan Watts

'Ah I get it! Life is experienced through thought. It's not going to help me lose this though is it?' (Grabs some belly fat). 'I mean this is reality… The doctor is saying this is a real issue…'

'Well I can see how it's true that experience comes and goes but the rent is due on Friday and I don't have the money. No amount of chat about awareness is going to make that go away.'

'Yes I see what you are saying that it is all inside out. Now could you give me a strategy of what to do if she bullies me again?'

The work I do is based on the fact that ultimately we are awareness of experience. Energy flows through the mind and experience changes accordingly. When we are in the experience of those problems that is all we can see. When we see that experience of problems, self, other people, everything as transient, we realise that the only constant is awareness. Seeing this, we have a completely different understanding.

Often someone asks about earning more money or losing weight or fixing a relationship and whether this coaching will sort out the issues they have. My truthful answer is that as we explore what is real these 'issues' disappear.

Because the truth is that there are no problems or issues out there.

And I don't mean in the sense of 'a problem is just an opportunity in disguise'. That is just a platitude that would have us sitting in a house, electricity cut off, saying 'well its good for the character'.

I mean it in the sense that any problem is only ever a thought believed. 100% of the time. As is an opportunity.

I'll pause for a moment while I (most of the time) and the entire world (except for those clear thinking souls among you) shout: *'This is ridiculous! Irresponsible! Of course there are problems out there!! At least 99 of them.'*

The thing is, there are no problems. And there are no opportunities. And there is no one to have problems or opportunities. As this becomes clearer, the problems we think we have to solve and the opportunities we think we have to chase and the idea of a person who has to solve and chase begins to fall away and simple, straightforward being takes their place.

Reality is a projection of thought believed.

From one belief to the next, the world is a great place or a difficult place.

People are there to help or obstruct.

Jobs are plentiful or we are living in a dystopian wasteland.

We are gorgeous or we should wear a paper bag on our head.

Doors are opening or they are banging shut in our face.

We are successful or a walking disaster.

And all variations in between, all changing from one moment to the next.

Any problem that we perceive is a creation of thought, fixed in place by beliefs. We know this because as thoughts and beliefs move on the problem is no longer there.

There are simple 'facts'. Like our bank balance or our waist measurement, the divorce papers on the desk or a diagnosis.

And every single aspect of those facts is held in thought. There is nothing inherent in an amount of money or a measurement or a piece of paper or some words from a doctor which is either bad or good, a curse or a blessing, a disaster or a miracle, significant or insignificant.

Which is why one moment it looks like we are depressed, stressed, anxious, frantic and desperate about something. The next moment we are not. The problem exists in one moment in time. Then energy shifts, thought flows through and life just happens, no problem in sight.

Thanks to thought believed we see problems, which in order to be problems have to come with a self that is stuck, a future in which suffering will occur and the belief that there is no solution. The self, the problem, the future and the lack of solution are inseparable, all clumped together in this experience. And none of it has any truth.

Attention is fixed on a difficult imagined future caused by a made up issue that by definition has no solution. Good luck with that one.

Hold on a minute, what are we saying here exactly?

Are we saying just forget about the debt and the divorce and the illness and the awful boss? Blank it all out and live in some crazed, fixed-smile Pollyanna land? The eternal sunshine of the head in the sand? Resolutely ignore the diet and the rent until it is a toss up whether the heart attack or the debt collector's dog gets us first?

This is the brilliance of who we really are. The truth of our nature, that once we realise it, means the end to stress, anxiety. The end to problems.

The fluidity of thought, the fact that problems appear and disappear from one moment to the next is the best reminder ever not to use any of that as our guide.

So what do we have instead to help us deal with the real world?

Ah. We have the most wonderful thing.

We have simple doing, the simple expression of life.

2. Doing

As we lose the panic and the imagined consequence of the 'problem', as the 'real' world reveals itself as not entirely, not very and then, not even slightly real, we start to notice what we are doing.

We are simply doing what makes sense for us. What we are doing is our integrity, our truth. It is nothing to do with what we 'should' do, or what is expected of us or what we can get away with. It is nothing to do with the panicked 'I HAVE TO SOLVE THIS OR ELSE WE ARE ALL DOOMED'. It is nothing to do with the stuff we are making up around the facts. It is nothing to do with trying to pin down an outcome.

This is where the universal meets the personal. The interface of truth and permanent to specific and momentary. Where formless comes into 'real' world form.

What we are doing right now is perfect. It is everything to do with the wisest, most expansive, most grounded way for us to live our life given our current understanding of who we are.

The more we see that there is nothing to do, just doing to observe, our frantic thoughts can settle. We start to get more real.

When someone struggling to pay the rent is no longer fixed in the dazzling headlights of what they are imagining, they see they are in simple reality. Breadth of vision widens. The reality seems to be the request for a sum of money. And if the person veers away from the simplest possible reality into what they think about that sum (huge! I'll never find it!) or about the consequences (we'll be eaten by rats!) then the stressful feelings will tell them they are off-track.

Out of the glare of the headlights and away from the shrill shriek of panic, they notice what they are doing. It might be asking for help. It might be moving house. It might be finding a way to earn more. Or speaking to the bank. Or not paying it. Or another simple, feasible, realistic doing, perfectly attuned to that individual in that moment of time, from an infinite supply of possibility.

This is our integrity. This is as real and clear as we can get. We never know what it will be. We will just notice we are doing it. We will just notice that we are free.

CLARE DIMOND

FREE TO SEE WHAT WE ARE DOING

FEAR

We are taught to not trust ourselves. We are taught fear. It doesn't come naturally to us.
Jeff Foster

Once upon a time, there was a beautiful young girl with long golden hair. Well… an average looking 35 year old with shortish brown hair. Her name was Mousy-locks.

Mousy-locks worked in marketing. She wasn't confident. She worried a lot. About many things. Speaking in front of people was always an ordeal for her. She feared all sorts of things: criticism, people laughing at her, getting things wrong, looking foolish or stupid…

Above all, though, she dreaded meetings with her boss's, boss's boss. He was roundish in shape with a grizzly brown beard. Mousy-locks was terrified of him. She did everything she could to avoid his bark of disapproval. Let's call him Boss-Bear.

Before a meeting with him she would have weeks of preparation, weeks of sleepless nights and then would sit in silence, sliding lower in her chair as he dismissed her proposal with a flick of his head or slammed a paw down on the table.

Then one day, Mousy-locks went on holiday to Canada, rounded a corner in a forest and came face to face with a bear. A real bear. A mother bear. Up on two legs, teeth bared, claws extended, two young cubs copying her. Mousy-locks and her husband backed away. They moved behind the corner, slowly got their bear spray cans out of their back packs and waited. After half an hour they moved tentatively forward again. The bear (let's call her Real Bear) was gone.

Back in the office, a meeting was scheduled with Boss Bear. Mousy Locks realised something was different. In Canada she had rounded a corner, stared a bear in the face, did what she did and was perfectly fine. In the office, what would happen to her? Being criticised? Not getting a promotion? Being shouted at or sacked. Strangely, none of it seemed a problem. She wasn't so afraid any more.

The End

Except it's not of course. Because many years later Mousy-locks started to explore the truth behind our experience and understood a bit more about Boss Bear and Real Bear.

She realised that in that moment in the Canadian forest, 100% present, no over-thinking or second guessing, a body had backed away, a hand had reached for the bear spray. There was nothing that she had to do.

She also realised that Boss Bear was a character in a story. Well there was a bearded person there in the room who was paid 750 times more than her but apart from that, she was pretty much making everything else up. And yes, ok, she was making up the money stuff as well. A whole long story about what he thought of her and what that imaginary opinion meant, what other people thought of what he said and what would be the consequences.

All of it was a carefully constructed story with a carefully constructed villain designed to keep the carefully constructed protagonist as the myth of a small mousey person who can't speak up in meetings, who can't be honest and free.

While all along, underneath the story, life was being lived.

So Mousy-locks kept exploring the nature of experience, along the way realising that fairy tales are great until you mistake them for what is actually going on. She changed her name to Clare Dimond and lived happily ever after.

The End

Not quite:

postscript 1: she hasn't been back to Canada yet but she definitely will.

postscript 2: she hasn't seen Boss Bear in a long time but would like to. She owes him an apology.

FREE TO TRUST

STRESS

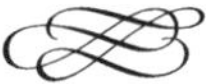

Everything that happens -- you never saw it coming. The greatest things in your life -- you did not predict; they simply unfolded...

Mooji

A client came to me with some goals that she wanted to work on through coaching. Not so unreasonable, you might be thinking.

And at one time, I would have jumped right into the goals with her, making sure they were SMART and all the rest of it, being there to encourage and spur her on.

But as we talked about her goals she told me how achieving them was important for her self-worth. She wanted to do them to prove herself to herself and to others, to show that she was valuable.

And that, I know now, is a ticket to striving and stress and never achieving fulfilment or worth. Because it will never be quite enough. There is always more to earn, more clients to gain, more articles to write, more marathons to run, more mountains to climb.

It is impossible to end a sense of lack and restriction through doing or acquiring. It is a bottomless pit or a never-ending trail.

Once we see who we are, this quest stops and life floods in.

It is useful to look at how we understand goals and how we respond to negative feelings. All of this is indicative of how clearly we understand who we really are.

When we believe that this idea of self is what we are, that there is no bigger picture, we believe we are on our own in this game. We believe there is tremendous responsibility on our shoulders. We work out of our intellect, acquiring more and more knowledge, working harder and harder and keeping an ever-tighter control. We make it about our personal discipline and commitment. This is the place I was in for most of my life, believing I had to prove myself to myself and to other people or lose everything. It is true that a lot can get done here, exams are passed, promotions happen, more money is earned, but the individual suffers through it.

When we are acting from this perspective, we use a goal as a symbol of our value and our character. As long as it involves some form of apparent progress, a goal is taken as a good thing simply because it is a goal. We don't have the insight to see that when we do things to save face or to impress others or to prove our value, we are only giving more credence to the thoughts that tell us we are unworthy or that we need to earn respect. We need to achieve the goal at all costs, and if we don't, we feel like a failure. Then, even when we achieve it, we still don't feel worthy or respected.

We believe that we make things happen through the pure

force of our will. There is a tension and restlessness that goes along with everything we do. It is about our identity as individuals. What we achieve reflects how worthy we are and how hard we can work. We are on a treadmill, and the minute we take a break, we lose our sense of who we are.

We force ourselves out of our comfort zone in order to grow, feeling the fear and stress the whole way. Indeed, we use stress and fear as an indication that the goal is worthy enough. Being comfortable or relaxed is a sign that we are not pushing ourselves hard enough, that we are lazy or uncommitted. We only deserve the good stuff that comes our way if we have worked hard for it. Stress is believed to be a sign that we are working hard and deserve the rewards.

Or the opposite is that we wait for the conditions in our mind and environment to be perfect before we will act.

The problem is that this is highly unlikely to happen.

There is a constant stream of thoughts going through our mind out of our control. If we wait for the mind to clear before we do anything then we could be waiting a very long time. This "waiting for the right feeling" becomes an excuse to avoid doing anything that seems to create insecurity.

We use stress and fear as a sign to do nothing or change direction. We feel that everything should align in harmony as a sign to act. Any negative feelings - anxiety, concern, fear - are taken seriously and acted on. We believe that stress is a sign to stop.

An alternative to all this is to simply watch the doing being done.

Action comes from deep within, with nothing on it other than the simple sense that it is being done. That in fact there is no choice about whether to do it. That if it is being done, it is for us to do. As we stay in a place of clarity, we know that if we find ourselves doing something else, we could instantly be part of that shift without any sense of failure.

Here, we know that stress and fear come and go. We know that mental state and insecurities are irrelevant. We simply live, using clarity, integrity and honesty to navigate. Simply doing what makes absolute sense to do, whether it is the washing up or making a speech to millions.

And these things that we are doing might before have seemed stressful. Now we just watch the doing occur, knowing that any thought of scale, or meaning, significance or outcome is only ever a thought believed.

FREE FROM PROVING OURSELVES.

CONFUSION

In times of pain, when the future is too terrifying to contemplate and the past too painful to remember, I have learned to pay attention to right now. The precise moment I was in was always the only safe place for me.
Julia Cameron, The Artist's Way

Sometimes we can seem so utterly confused that it looks like we have no idea of how to move forward. We don't even know what to do let alone have the freedom to act on it.

A few years ago, I found myself in a state of total overwhelm. My head was in chaos. I couldn't sleep or really eat. I couldn't pretend to be my normal self with friends so I avoided company. I was shaking, exhausted and low. I was looking into the future and all I saw were bleak, desolate choices which had nothing to do with the life I desired. I was looking at the past and seeing how things were not at all as I had thought they were. I felt I was living on quicksand. Everything – past, present and future – seemed jumbled, awful and desperate.

People in my practice sometimes talk about feeling absolutely overwhelmed. Sometimes, something has happened, an event that seems to have pulled the rug out from underneath their life. Or sometimes nothing has happened and they have gradually become more and more stuck or confused or tired. Everything seems so hopeless. It is impossible to believe that there is a way out.

There were many moments when I felt like that, when it was absolutely beyond me to think that things could be different. There didn't seem to be any options or possibility.

All I really knew to do during these moments was to keep breathing. So I kept breathing. Sometimes my head cleared enough to notice that I could breathe. At other times my thoughts were so whirling and painful that all I could do was live in the full confusion.

Breathe. I knew to do it.

It was one small breadcrumb on the tangled ground of an immense, chaotic forest. All around it were weeds and thorns but there it was, one single breadcrumb. I knew to breathe. That was it. It wasn't much but it was enough. I knew to do it. I knew how to do it. It was obvious and clear and it made sense. It was all I had.

And I stayed with the breathing. And in staying with the breathing, I could see the next breadcrumb. In staying with what I knew to do, I had put myself on a path and on the path was another breadcrumb. I picked it up. As I picked it up, I knew that the crying I was already doing made sense. I didn't try to stop it. So I cried. It made sense to cry.

And because I was doing something that made sense to do, I could see the next breadcrumb.

I picked it up and I knew to speak to someone I trusted. It was a terribly hard conversation to have but I knew to do it. It was just one breadcrumb, one small thing.

I did that small thing that made sense right then and that opened the path a bit wider. The next breadcrumb became slightly more obvious. Then there was another. Then another. And gradually by following these breadcrumbs I emerged from the chaos.

And this is all we can ever do when our head is so full and our reality is upside down and our mind is numb or racing. Look for the first breadcrumb. It will be there and it will be there just for you. What makes sense for anyone else is irrelevant. There will be something there that is just for you.

It might be an action to take. Perhaps just to notice the wisdom that is already keeping you alive like breathing or eating or drinking.

It might be to continue doing what you are doing right now – crying, shouting, raging, sitting.

Or it might be a non-action action like resting or stopping work or no more crying or shouting or doing nothing or not seeing anyone.

Or it might be to stand up or sit down or open a window or go outside.

It might take you in the direction of a connection. Perhaps a connection to yourself and something you know to be true.

Or it might suggest a connection to another person or an

animal or to a place or a book or a poem or a piece of music or water.

It won't promise anything. It will never say 'do this and everything will be sorted out.' Because this is about your expansion and growth and your realisation of who you are. What you can see in this moment, however useful it is right now, will not apply as you rise up the mountain. It will simply say 'This makes sense right now'.

And in this action or non action, connection to self or other that makes sense right now we open up a space. We shift our view by a fraction of a degree so that what we are looking at now isn't quite the same as it was, there is something slightly different. And breadcrumb by breadcrumb, fraction of a degree by fraction of a degree we move forwards towards the clearing.

There are more of us than we could ever imagine, seemingly stuck in chaos or trapped in numb confusion. However hopeless it seems though, there is always that one bread-crumb, that one small thing that we know to do. One tiny crumb in a world of whatever turmoil or disillusion we are experiencing.

It is not much but it is always enough. It is always there. And there will always be another.

FREE TO TAKE THE TINY NEXT STEP

INSECURITY

The splitting of the atom has changed everything, except for how we think.
Albert Einstein

Energy ebbs and flows. The mind moves from a low state to a high state randomly and continuously. This is simply the natural flow of life. The tide moving in and out. Inhale and exhale. Systole and diastole. The move through autumn from summer to winter and into spring. Day into night. Life into death into a different form of life into death again. That constant movement and change. We are part of it. Of course, the energy of mind ebbs and flows. It is impossible for it not to.

And that ebb and flow is generated by whatever generates the pull and push of universal energy. It has nothing to do with us. Just as the tide has nothing to do with the water. Impersonal.

Now, because most of us don't understand that energy goes

up and down of its own accord and states of mind go up and down accordingly and thoughts change, we believe there has to be a reason for our changing feelings. And of course we look outside, to the outside world to explain to us why we are feeling high or low in a particular moment.

And this fundamental misunderstanding leads us into...

The hamster wheel of insecurity (I made that name up myself...)

The energy dips in our mind and we feel low – depressed or anxious or unhappy. We believe that something must have caused those low feelings. We look outside for an explanation.

And because we have certain beliefs about ourselves and certain thought patterns, these create a lens through which we project an outside world, a well-worn channel through which our attention flows.

We look out into the world and find an explanation of our low mood that corresponds to what we think we know about ourself and the world.

And it looks so real. Because right in front of us is the evidence. A client has cancelled. I've been left out of a party. My rumpled ugly face in the mirror. A driver cutting me up. No wonder I'm feeling inadequate, rejected, ugly or insulted. The reason is obvious! I knew it all along! People don't like me. I'm not attractive. Drivers are aggressive. No wonder I am insecure. How can I ever fulfil my potential in this insecure world?

But we forget that we are not seeing straight. We forget that, in fact, it is impossible for us to see straight. We can never,

ever, ever, ever see ourselves or the world for what it is. Whatever we see is 100% dictated, coloured, shaped and carved out by what we believe about ourselves and the world, our thought patterns and tendencies and by the state of mind we are in at that precise moment.

The crazily logical thing is that when we mistake this creation of personal beliefs and mood for actual reality, we react to it as if it were real and, in the reaction, we create the very thing we are resisting.

If I believe I am unattractive, I will see evidence I am unattractive. I will believe this evidence. I'll hide myself away. I'll stop smiling. I'll suspect that the people who chat to me just feel sorry for me. I'll withdraw. This will feed my low mood. I'll see more evidence. And on and on. In other words, I will make myself into the most unattractive version of myself. I see what was only ever a projection and I turn it into a self-continuing experience of apparent reality.

If I believe people don't like me, I will seek out evidence that people don't like me. I'll react to and dwell on any perceived slight. I'll be rude to them. I'll be ultra-sensitive and frosty or needy. I'll make myself as unlikeable as I can be.

If I believe drivers are careless and inconsiderate, I will look for evidence that drivers are inconsiderate. I'll see people cutting me up and not giving way. I'll beep at them, scowl, push ahead, show them they can't ignore me on the roads. I'll be living in a dream in which other drivers will react accordingly to my poor, inconsiderate driving.

It is the same with every single thing that we see 'out there'.

It is an utterly vicious circle. Our thoughts create the reality that we want to escape from or change. Whatever we resist persists. It has to. There is no other way it can work. The whole thing takes on a life of its own. The invented becomes the even more apparently real.

Seeing the truth of this is utterly transformational. It is this understanding that allows us to step out of the hamster wheel and into who we really are, into what is actually going on.

When we really see that state of mind fluctuates all the time, we start realising that what is seen out in the world is just a function of universal energy.

We realise that problems or opportunities, exclusion or invitations, an ugly or a beautiful face in the mirror, helpful or unhelpful people depends entirely on how thoughts are directed by a state of mind and habitual patterns and beliefs in that moment.

None of it is real in any true sense. When we realise the infinite amount of swirling energy out there, it is impossible that what is being noticed is anything more than a single, filtered pixel in an immense ever-changing, impossible to define landscape.

And this realisation breaks the cycle. We see it all for what it is and we realise the blinkered madness of creating the very thing that contradicts what deep down we know ourselves to be. It is impossible for us to react anymore. Because we know there is nothing there to react against. The insecurity reveals itself to be no more substantial, permanent or real than a mirage.

When we know not to look outside any more for any version of reality, all we can do is look to the entirety of the experience, to notice how life works, to see who we really are.

With this understanding, it doesn't matter in the slightest what our state of mind is doing, whether we are breathing in or out, whether we feel desperate insecurity or utter calm. There is no self to defend and protect.

There is just life and awareness of life.

Hamster wheel going cheap to first bidder. Anyone…? Anyone…?

FREE TO STEP OFF THE WHEEL

ACCEPTANCE

Get your facts first.
Then you can distort them as you please.
Mark Twain

Acceptance is a funny old word.

I gave a talk once and mentioned acceptance. A young man spoke up. He said, 'I really get the idea of acceptance. I can do that really well. I live with my friend and every morning when I open the fridge to get milk for cereal I see that he has drunk almost all the milk the night before. And so I have accepted that he is a selfish b*****d who doesn't give a flying f**k about me and my breakfast. I've accepted that.'

That wasn't quite what I had in mind.

But it opened up a good discussion. Because the big question when it comes to acceptance is WHAT ARE WE ACCEPTING?

Anything we think we have to accept isn't what we have to accept. The terrible events, the annoying people, the difficult circumstances. All of these will change as mental energy changes. One moment looking like disasters separating us from the life we want and the next appearing as something else altogether.

And yet, however they appear, in that moment of appearance, they are real to us.

Take the young man with the friend and the milk (or rather not much of a friend apparently and very little milk). In that moment, next to the fridge, he believed the thoughts going through his mind that said his friend was selfish and didn't care about him. In that moment, that was reality. And when it came to acceptance that is what it looked like he had to accept. A selfish friend who couldn't care less about him.

We know though that with any change of perspective or belief, he would have a different experience. He would be looking out on a different world altogether. He could experience a friend who is oblivious or forgetful or absent minded or generous and kind in every other way or simply thirsty rather than selfish. He could laugh and make sure he gets extra milk in for tomorrow. He could experience a friend that he loves unconditionally who he would gladly give anything in the world to - including all the milk and maybe even all the coffee.

With even a slight space between us and the experience we move from seeing it as real to seeing it as real IN THAT MOMENT. This is huge. When we realise the truth of this, that experiences are only ever real in the moment they are being experienced, we see that all we ever have to accept is the fact of experience, awareness of experience.

We never have to accept the content of that experience because that is constantly changing. To try to accept the content is to say 'This is how I am. This is how they are. This is how life is.' Not only can it not possibly be true. It also for that moment has us living in an illusion of being absolutely stuck, of the impossibility of change.

Trying to force ourselves to accept what looks absolutely real and absolutely awful only sets us up for an impossible task and a load of self blame. 'I just have to accept that it is really shit and they hate me' - who can possibly do that?

When we understand this more clearly, we accept the fact that experience will always change. We accept that all emotions, all thoughts are possible. We accept that control over any of it is impossible and, anyway, unnecessary. We accept the simple mind blowing truth of who we are.

FREE TO ACCEPT

STORIES

When our thoughts look real, we live in a world of suffering. When they look subjective, we live in a world of choice. When they look arbitrary, we live in a world of possibility. And when we see them as illusory, we wake up inside a world of dreams.

Michael Neill

A client emailed me to tell me she had left her job.

What will she say when I ask her why? I wondered. Something like:

"It didn't make me happy"?

"I really don't like the people"?

"The politics were toxic"?

"They didn't make me feel secure"?

Or will she pause for a while, search for a reason, and then shrug and say, "It's weird. I actually don't know why. It just made sense to leave."

Same action. The only difference is a story about it or not.

Getting married, beginning a project, starting a job, creating a friendship, initiating a programme or trying out a sport . . .

Or staying married, completing a project, continuing in a job, keeping a friendship, running a programme or staying with a sport . . .

Or divorcing a spouse, quitting a project, resigning a job, ending a friendship, ditching a programme or stopping a sport . . .

We start, continue or stop any or all of these. That is out of our control. It looks like it is decided by this small independent being we believe ourselves to be but it is not.

But we make up a story about the apparent decision. A story about securing our happiness or avoiding unhappiness or feeling more secure or more successful or less fearful, or making people love, respect or admire us or because we feel we should.

All of these are fabrications. There is no fixed truth in any of this.

Or we can realise that we seem to be starting, continuing or stopping. And that anything we think about it is an after thought.

Believing that our own small personal mind is in control, we explain the doing (which is happening regardless) with whatever story fits our state of mind and conditioned thinking.

But when we see this more clearly, we know that we are the pure awareness of a body being moved, of words being formed, of food being cooked, of love being made, of kids being cared for.

As ultimate creativity, freshness and inspiration, we witness the miracle of life. We watch the film unfold knowing it is perfect. It is a miraculous story enough in its own right. There is no need to add in the drama of suffering or resistance.

We move from being caught up in the film of an 'I' that believes it decides to awareness of unlimited being and doing.

And as we notice this movement, backwards and forwards as the tide goes in and out, we realise it doesn't matter even slightly where we are in it. It doesn't matter if the tide is high up on the beach or far out. Both are equally perfect. It is the same with us. Believing this idea of a self and a world or understanding that self and world are experiences within consciousness.

No matter how stuck we have been in the mire of our insecure thinking, there is always this moment now, fresh. And this moment contains the possibility to drop the suffering contained in an idea of a separate self.

There is never a moment that does not contain the possibility of insight, no matter what has gone before.

There is never a moment in which we aren't moving between the two vastly separate worlds of illusion or clarity.

There is never a moment when where we are matters.

FREE TO SIMPLIFY

THIS

You only are free when you realise you belong no place — you belong every place — no place at all.
Maya Angelou

A fundamental misunderstanding is that the world or a person or an object has the ability to make us feel good or bad. If good, then we desire more of it. If bad, then we desire less.

When we believe the world has the power to make us feel good, there is never enough of what we need.

When we believe the world has the power to make us feel bad, there is always too much of what we fear.

When we see that there is no world out there to cause an effect and no self to feel good or bad, there is only this. And the 'this' is pure magic.

Never enough

If I believe that my life circumstances determine whether I feel good or worthy or safe or valuable or even simply OK, then I will continually look to the outside world to feed my need to maintain the best possible circumstances.

And nothing I do will ever be enough.

There will never be enough of whatever it is I think I desire to make me feel OK.

If I believe I need money to make me feel secure, I will never have enough money; and the money I do I have, I will worry about losing.

If I believe I need someone to tell me they love me so I feel loved, they can never tell me enough times.

If I believe I need approval to make me feel appreciated, I will never have enough approvers. I will never have enough upvotes of my answer, likes of my page, five star ratings of my book. (Feel free to give this book five stars, by the way.)

If I believe I need people to defer to me in order to make me feel important, there will never be enough people deferring to me.

If I believe I need food in the cupboard to make me feel I won't go hungry, there will never be enough food.

If I believe I need friends to make me feel wanted, I will never have enough friends.

If I believe I need to change how I look in order to be beautiful, I will never be able to change enough.

This is a life in which I feel that I need to force myself through obstacles and out of comfort zones. I need to make more effort, have more willpower, force, charm, charisma, determination, strategy and expertise to secure what it is I think I require in order to feel OK.

From this place, I might well be expanding out in the world —collecting more money, property, promotions, friends, lovers, awards, food, fans, reviews, employees in order to feel OK. It might look to other people that I am having a ball. It might look like I have life nailed down.

But, I know in my heart that I am looking for something that I can't seem to find no matter how much I acquire.

It is like building a mansion on a foundation of quicksand, adding extra wings and rooms and extensions in the attempt to feel OK. And it will never be grand enough or majestic enough for me to feel OK about myself.

It is never enough.

**

Too much

THE OTHER SIDE of the coin is the belief that circumstances, things and other people can make me feel bad.

When I think things in the outside world have the power to make me feel bad, overloaded, fearful, insecure then I will embark on a life of avoidance or control. I will seek to manage and minimise these things, protect myself from them.

This is where the comfort zone rules supreme. And where it gets smaller and smaller until I am living on a pinhead, barricaded off from anything that I believe has the power to disturb me.

If I think my to-do list is causing me stress, then I will believe I need to have less to do. I will seek to avoid having things to do until I have nothing to do.

If I think that certain people can upset, annoy or offend me, then I will either seek to avoid them or, if I have the power, seek to banish them from my world as I retract into my shell.

If I think that certain places can make me uncomfortable, I will avoid those places until I am living in the island of my country, town, house, bedroom or bed.

If I think certain activities have the power to scare me or make me insecure, I will limit what I do to the most-familiar repetitions.

This is the step-by-step shrinking of my world and of myself. Believing that the world can disturb me and that I must not be disturbed, I need to limit, narrow, reduce, control and minimise.

It is all too much.

***

Anything

Then one day, I realise something about the nature of life. I realise that everything experienced is transitory. Indeed, that the 'I' itself in the experience is also changing constantly.

None of these things, this idea of self or other have any power.

I look around at the world and at the self. It all looked so real before. It all looked as though it had the ability to make life a heaven or hell.

Now I see that, but for thought believed, there is nothing there. It is thought that provides the opinions, the likes and dislikes, the preferences, the fears, the desires. And that all of these come and go from moment to moment.

Sometimes, they seem to matter. Sometimes, they don't. Sometimes there is nothing there but pure marvel at the aliveness.

I realise that I am gazing out into nothing. Blank canvases that are brought alive, animated, given colour by thought and belief. Nothing out there can create worth or value. None of it can create sadness or discomfort.

I realise that, because of the power of thought to create any experience, all experience is equal and transient. Any person. Any colleagues. Any job. Any house. Any climate. Any style. Any country. All experienced through thought.

Anything or nothing or everything.

We are wide open to whatever appears.

Anything.

***

This

And then a strange thing happens.

The anything and the nothing and the everything give rise to the simplicity of living, being, doing. Consciousness watches as apparent choices are made.

From the "any one" come our soulmates.

It could be the person we have been married to and arguing with for ten years who we now see with different eyes. It could be someone else. Awareness is in love with everyone, and out of that love emerge the most special of people.

From the "any job" comes a calling.

It could be the job we have always done in which we now realise enormous possibility or something else altogether. From an infinite choice of jobs and careers, a particular path appears that is so compelling, so exciting and so obvious there is no choice about what to do.

From the "any country, town or street" comes the right country, town or street for right now.

It could be where we are living now that we come home to with a previously unknown appreciation, or it might be on the other side of the world. In love with the whole world, the place for now is obvious.

From the "any way of life" comes the perfect way of life for right now.

It could be exactly as we are living, or it could change in every single detail. Knowing we can live in any way we want, we live in the way that makes simple, perfect sense.

Having seen the power of thought to create an illusory world, we are now guided from within, from integrity, truth, simplicity, to create a real world beyond our wildest dreams. We move and act with a freedom and a love and a whole mind, body and soul participation. With a full heart, we love the people we are with, the jobs we do, the places we live.

There is no meaning that has to be extracted. There is nothing that has to prove us or make us feel secure. There is nothing for us to pin down or rely on.

We are living, creating, experiencing and loving with an authenticity, peace, expansion and joy we never thought possible.

FREE TO KNOW

COMFORT ZONE

Not a single person is born in the world who has not a certain capacity which will make him proud, who is not pregnant with something to produce, to give birth to something new and beautiful, to make the existence richer. There is not a single person who has come into the world empty.

Osho

Inevitably, as we see more clearly that we are ultimately awareness of experience, we become increasingly comfortable with feeling uncomfortable.

All of those thoughts about our limits, about what people will think, about getting it wrong that used to floor us before still come and go. We still feel them, it's just that the legs have been kicked out from underneath them. We just can't take them as seriously as we used to.

Because we know deep down that it means absolutely nothing. It is transient. Here one minute. Gone the next.

All the hateful, peaceful, angry, insecure, secure, anxious, calm, up and down thinking is just the changing energy flowing through and our unconscious attachment of illusory specifics to that energy.

This stream of thought says nothing about the world, about us, about other people. No matter how real or chock full of vital information it seems to be. It tells us absolutely nothing. Zilch.

The outcome is that we can get very very very comfortable with being uncomfortable.

We can feel it all physically. Observe as the raging extremes of nerves, fear, anger, hatred roll through us. Our hands can clench and tremble. Our stomachs can flip and clench. Our foreheads can tense and ache. The only information in any of it is that thoughts are passing through.

We can notice it all and still just see that we are doing what we are doing, fully aware that transient experience, ultimately, is nothing to do with who we are.

And the ironic next thing to happen, is that all this being comfortable with discomfort means the beginning of the end of the comfort zone.

Let's take a moment to say goodbye to this supposed refuge that has accompanied us from the moment the first thought of 'I' and a separate world entered our heads. And let's consider why its time has come.

The comfort zone is the place the 'I' believes it has to retreat to when it feels inadequate or when the outside world seems scary. In the comfort zone are the things that the 'I' believes it can do, experience or say without the risk of looking foolish. Here are the people it believes it can talk to and the places it can go without risk. This is the place where it believes it can be secure.

Then there is everything outside the comfort zone which is off-limits. The no-go area of life. We can see it all as we peek out from under the blankets but the thought of venturing out into it…? Oh no.

We should make the most of it as long as it lasts. Because the very first insight we have into the transient, illusory nature of this idea of who we are is the very first nail in the coffin of the comfort zone.

There is no other way.

The more obvious it is that everything we see changes all the time, the more we stop looking outside for the guide of what to do. The more we simply notice what we are doing.

And this noticing is like an internal GPS.

There are the nudges and the prompts and the 'why are you making such a big deal of this?' that tells us to just get on with what we know to do.

There are the winces, the pain and the discomfort that tell us we are out of alignment with our deepest integrity.

There are the moments when we see everything. We are clear, in love with it all.

There are light-up-the-sky bursts of inspiration. The alchemy of individual and universal that allow us to create, think, say, embody and write the original and transcendent. This is what my coach Garret Kramer calls the 'impersonal cool stuff' that inevitably shows up the more clearly we see through the idea of the personal.

This has always been there. Who we really are has never changed. It is just that before we were too busy trying to find a solution to imaginary problems to take any notice.

Now we are no longer so tangled up. We are not spending our time constructing new convoluted tunnel extensions to the rabbit warren of thought.

We are looking inwards. There is no other viable direction to look.

And now, when we have the insight or the inspiration or the deep inner knowing or the nudge or the prompt we can try retreating into the comfort of 'I'm not brave/intelligent/rich enough to do that' or 'I would do it but the world/that person is too mean/scary/busy/competitive right now.'

But it sits so badly with us. It is as though we are trying to squeeze ourselves into a coat or a pair of shoes that we are out-growing by the minute.

Now that we have seen this insecure thinking for the transient energy it is and now that we have seen the inner flame, nudges and certainty for the movement of life they really are, our 'comfort zone' is laughable.

Staying here, pretending to believe insecure thoughts, pretending not to notice our inner truth is like trying to hide a floodlight with a piece of gauze or put out a bonfire with a sheet of tissue paper.

We know what to do. We do what we do and sometimes we drop into the true freedom that we really are. This freedom is pure excellence—true, loving, expansive, authentic, inspired and resolute. And we know that anything that gets in the way is transient, insubstantial, ever changing illusion.

Live out the excellence at our very core?

Or suffer as we pretend to believe the illusion.

Not much of a choice is it?

FREE TO EXCEL

COMMENTARY

Cease connecting your well-being to objects, relationships, or status.
Cease connecting your resilience to anything that changes, appears, disappears, or comes and goes.
Cease connecting your security to anything that, by nature, is insecure.
Cease connecting the freedom of who you truly are to who you truly are not.
Garret Kramer

"And here she comes up on the left side. She's had a bad season so she probably doesn't have it in her. Plus she's been eating too much chocolate and so she's not going to even fit in the dress she bought for the event this weekend. AND she's going to it on her own so not only will she be not fitting into her dress, she will be standing like a lemon in a corner. What she should do now is to not eat and exercise all week. And be better at keeping husbands. Oh look now another chocolate bar. What a loser. She really should get a grip. And she missed the kids' dentist appointment. What sort of crap mother is she? She should be better at stuff like that. Everyone else can do it. What an absolute loser…"

And on and on and on and on and on and on and on and on.

That's what the commentary on the inside of my head has been like. (Apart from the bit about coming up on the left side. I just put that in to show off my sports knowledge.)

And this commentary is relentless. Sometimes it ramps up so intensely it's like the guy who does the Grand National. Hyped up, hysterical, barely comprehensible, not pausing for breath.

Now the interesting thing is that while this commentary has been having a field day slamming the loser, the 'loser' has just been doing what it does - breathing, moving, talking, working, tidying, picking kids up, cooking, reading, sleeping. It is doing the same whether the commentary thinks it is the best thing since sliced bread, or, like now, the scum of the earth.

There is life apparently happening. And there is a non-stop dramatic analysis of life happening.

There is the game. And there is the commentary on the game.

And that's the design. It's a great design. Many of us like listening to the commentary on a match. It is entertainment. Engaging. All those opinions and stories and stats, comparisons and head shaking, tutting and nodding in appreciation, all that leaping around and punching the air and outrage and 'send him off'. All that drama and tension.

We watch and listen to the commentary in full knowledge that it does not change the game in any way. Reality.

But, in our lives, with our own commentary box, we are insane. We turn the whole thing upside down. We believe that the commentary is the game. We believe that listening to or changing or making the commentary wiser, more informed or more positive will make the game a different game. That it will somehow improve the actual play or secure a win for the right side or bring home the trophy.

And this is ridiculous. For so many reasons this is ridiculous.

The commentary in our minds, like the commentary on tv, is only ever an after-action description. It is post. It is always playing catch up.

It has no control or predictive powers. It cannot choose what is happening now. It cannot say what will happen in one second's time let alone a year, let alone ten years.

Its view-point is necessarily, infinitesimally narrow, honing in on a few tiny microscopic details in an infinite ocean of details that could also have been noticed.

It is ridiculously distorted. Layer upon layer of beliefs, prejudices, fears, insecurities, expectations, judgements make seeing clearly, even this small slither, impossible.

It pulls in random, meaningless comparisons as benchmarks. Leaping into the past, into others lives. Making it all up as if it had power to remember and see.

Not one single word it says is true. Every single thing can be flipped to the opposite and be just as valid. Not one single word is true.

This commentary is not reality. Not even close.

And all the while, in reality, the game is just doing its thing.

So what is the outcome of seeing this?

Firstly, we realise that the commentary is not the key to life. That is never the place to put our attention. It can never be accurate, can never change the game in any way. We see it for what it is. Inconsequential drama.

Secondly, without the need to appease the commentators, there is no need to change the game. The game is happening as it happens. Pure breath-taking perfection. After all any thought or judgement of something wrong could only ever come from the guys in their commentary box with their narrow, distorted, unreliable opinions.

As we stop putting effort into changing the inconsequential and irrelevant or trying to change the unchangeable and the perfect, we are freed up. We see who we really are. We are not the commentators. We are not even the game.

We are the space in which it all takes place. All of it is who we are, all of it brought alive by us. We see the breath-taking magnificence of the whole thing. The way it fits. We see every shining, sparkling detail. Hear every note. Feel everything it is possible to feel. All of it is us. It is impossible for anything to be better than this. Impossible for anything to be better than who we are.

We realise this. And then we hear the commentary box start up…

Remembering who we are, we notice the innocent confused self-importance of the commentary box. Its sweet, crazy idea that it is running the show. Its search for home.

It can do what it wants, say what it wants. All of it comes from love. Can be received with love.

We remember who we are. Our vision expands. We see everything.

FREE TO SEE

OUTCOME

The most important thing is that you don't identify yourself as being the doer of actions.
Mooji

All our lives we believe we have to be better, happier, more productive, higher earning, more educated, more successful, more popular, more impactful, different in some way. We resist what is and we seek the other.

So it would be very natural and logical for us to use our understanding of who we are to make things better – whether that is a relationship, our bank balance, our business, our health, our neighbourhood...

Can this understanding get us on the right track? Can we use our understanding that we are pure love and pure intelligence to impress a customer, to be a better parent or get on better with our colleagues.

The answer is no.

Because this 'right track', this customer, this friend, this role of parent, those colleagues are experience of thought brought alive through consciousness.

We believe that something said or done is right, wrong, better, worse, perfect, terrible, helpful, unhelpful simply according to the movement of thought flowing through us. There is nothing objective or stable or true about it.

So the only effect of the 'outcome' is to send us straight back into the illusion. We end up using our understanding of the illusion to get more lost in it, believing there is some reality to it, that one way is better than another, that there is an insightful right way to speak to someone or to do things and a confused wrong way.

If the only truth is that we are formless energy in an ever changing thought created consciousness then there cannot ever be a right and wrong, better or worse, helpful or unhelpful, more insightful or less insightful.

There is only ever experience delivered through thought.

It sends us round in circles if we try to use clarity as to the illusory nature of life to be better at the illusion.

It only makes sense to use our understanding of the illusory nature of life to understand the illusory nature of life.

Full stop.

And that is the crazy, magnificent, mind-blowing beauty of the whole thing. With the full stop, several things happen:

1. We truly don't fear any experience

The 'in order to' contains within it the need for something to go a certain way, it contains judgement, risk, fear, preference, control... Again, totally understandable, but utterly inconsistent with what is really happening.

If we really saw that all experience was created from thought in the moment then we would not try to change that experience. We would be the truth of what we are: awareness in apparent human form experiencing.

All of it – every thought, every feeling, every experience is simply how it is. There is nothing to change.

As we realise that no experience is better than any other, we become who we really are: a being let loose in the most exciting playground in the universe. We realise there is nothing we need to do there is just the sheer fascination of the experience.

2. The 'must be done'

In the freedom of seeing through the 'in order to' we see the 'what must be done'. This is only ever the obvious thing to do. It is free of reasons why. It is free of 'shoulds' and 'ought to's' and 'trying'. It is as free from the illusion of thought that we can get while living in a thought created reality.

It is, essentially, what we cannot stop ourselves from doing.

I am breathing because I can't stop myself from breathing. I am not breathing in order to stay alive or to be healthier. I am just breathing.

At 4pm I will be picking up my kids from school because I literally cannot stop myself from picking them up. I am not picking them up so that I can be a better parent or because I want them to like me. I am picking them up because I can't stop myself from doing that.

I am writing this book because I can't stop myself from writing this book. (Believe me I have a million other things that I 'should' be doing). I am not writing it because I love writing it. I am not writing for any response because I know any response is my experience of thought in the moment. I am writing it because I can't not write it.

"But I only have one life." you might say "I want to go to Asia and own a Tesla and live in a nice house and stay healthy. To do this I need to earn money or exercise. Sometimes I will have to do what I don't want to do in order to have all this."

And immediately we are plunged back in the illusion of a thought created reality. When we are out of the illusion we realise we are just doing what we are doing because that is what we are doing.

The same is true for all of it. Buying a Tesla, going to Asia, cleaning the house, paying the bills, writing the novel, climbing Everest, going to work, standing in front of a column of tanks, refusing to give up a seat on the bus for a white person.

We will be doing it because we can't stop ourselves from doing it. We are doing what must, from the inner most, simplest, most obvious place, be done.

The other side of the full stop.

And this takes us to the other side of the full stop.

It looks like we cannot escape our human form other than through death. Yet we know, while still alive, without question that we are more than this human form. We are so so much more than our fears and worries and insecurities. We are so much more even than our talents, our best relationships, our skills.

Trying to use our knowledge of the spiritual to get better at being a human keeps us firmly stuck in the illusory limits of the human. It takes away the relief of the full stop and adds a whole series of infinite made up reasons about made up people in made up situations needing made up things.

The full stop puts paid to all that. We pause. We mark a space. We take a breath and look at the marvel of what comes next.

Because the other side of the full stop is where it all happens.

The other side of the full stop is where clarity about why we do what we do begins. We know that we are here in human form. We know that experience has to be through the form or otherwise it would not take place. It has to be through our ears, eyes, taste buds, skin.

And instead of using this human form to get stuck in the personal, the individual, the prosaic. We use it to transcend it. This is the gift of human personal life when we use it to see the infinite and universal. This is the sheer beauty of what happens when we do not fear experience, of when we drop the 'in order to'.

The form is vital. A human, a pair of running shoes and a track. A pen, piece of paper and a hand. A stage, a voice, four words. A board room, a team, a suggestion. A rocket and an astronaut. A car, a mum, two kids at 4pm...

And something is created *through that form* that transports us momentarily *out of the form*. Through the individual we move out of the illusion of the individual. Through the everyday, obvious simple 'must be done' we move into the infinite, unknowable, indescribable freedom of who we are.

FREE OF OUTCOMES

THE FACTORY SETTING

And once this seeker, that always thinks it has to find something and discover something new or different falls away, suddenly there is a total relaxation and dropping into the sheer joy of being this.
Tony Parsons

My son and I were building the free toy that he got with his lego magazine (or rather the very expensive toy attached to a few bits of paper but anyway.)... It was some sort of spider thing with a top half that revolved. He put it all together but when he turned the top it knocked the legs so they fell off.

We paused. I had a momentary thought of, 'This is weird. Really? A less than perfect lego design...?' As veteran builders of many many lego toys, though, we both realised in a split second that we had missed something in the instructions. We checked and indeed there was a piece still in the bag which, once in its correct position, raised the top high enough that it could turn without touching the spider legs.

How could we have possibly thought that there might be

something wrong with the design? This is lego. In all the hundreds (thousands? He is already six after all) of boxes we have built together, there has never even been the tiniest of pieces missing let alone a whole instruction left out.* It could only ever have been us momentarily not noticing something.

It seems that, as it is with lego, so it is with who we are. The perfection of the design. Nothing ever missing. Nothing ever wrong. Just sometimes a bit of confusion, an oversight, easily put right, and then straight back into awareness of the perfection.

Our design is pure consciousness. Loving, intelligent, joyful, peaceful, unlimited consciousness. This is what we are. Living being. Magnificent and all-encompassing .

Within this consciousness that we are, a thought appears and is believed. This is the thought of an I, a 'me'.

This thought of an 'I' becomes the idea of a personal mind, a separate individual, limited and distinct.

Into this personal mind crowd other thoughts and beliefs. Thoughts of other people and money and work and politicians and the weather and work and decisions to make and obstacles and lego sets.

For all of these to exist in the way they seem to exist, the 'I' has to first appear as a thought and be believed. Because all of these other thoughts are only ever in relation to the 'I'.

Preferences, meanings, assumptions, perceptions, implications, significance - all connected to this idea of 'I'. (Ironically, even the thought of 'nothing to do with me' can only be experienced in relation to the 'I'.)

There are moments when there is no thought of an 'I', no personal mind. In deep sleep for example. Or in those moments when we have this crazy, profound falling away of self and realisation of life. Or in moments of absolute absorption or immersion. No reference to self. No reference to other. No reference to objects. No limits. No physical boundary. Just purest awareness. Just life.

There are moments when the experience of this 'I' perfectly matches the truth of its origin. The personal, thought-created but real-looking world resonates in deep accordance with who this 'I' really is.

These moments are when the 'I' realises that any experience, any thought, any feeling is a miracle of being. This is the 'I' in line with its true nature. It is life and in love and free and in tune with itself.

When the 'I' knows its true origin, then these moments are wonderful, breath-taking and also inevitable, constant.

The 'I' knows they are simply the natural result of an idea of an 'I' that is love, peace, intelligence, freedom and joy at its very core. That the thought-created world is only ever a reflection of that knowledge.

Knowing it is peace, love, joy, intelligence and potential, that is all it can see.

In the moments when it forgets its origin, moments of peace, love, freedom or joy seem like gasps of air to someone who is drowning. These moments seem to be the only place where life is real, where truth is to be found and yet they appear transient, dependent on things that look outside of control.

There is desperation in the attempts to recreate these moments - clinging to partners, seeking thrills, controlling, escapism, using substance and activity to obliterate the pain of having forgotten.

This 'I', in the moments that it forgets its origin, must avoid anything that shakes this idea of 'I ', because it believes that is all it has. It looks like there is nothing else. It tries to avoid rejection, failure and isolation not knowing that rejection, failure and isolation are impossibilities.

The personal mind of the 'I', forgetting who it is, believes thoughts of hatred, anger, despair and restriction. These thoughts are then what the 'I' has to live out as if they are real.

The sense of 'something's wrong here' can cause us to question the design, embark on a never-ending search to recreate and pin down the good things in life. Or it can be a reminder that, for a moment, we have forgotten we are life itself.

These moments of forgetting are simply the overlooked piece, safely waiting for us in the lego bag. All that is ever needed is the reminder of it.

The design is perfect. The instructions are perfect. All the pieces left the factory. Perfect. Just sometimes a little bit of confusion. A moment of doubt. A forgetting. Then perfection, freedom, love realised again.

FREEDOM IS THE DESIGN

**when I shared this chapter a friend said that once he had a lego set with a piece missing. He wrote to lego and they sent a new one. So maybe occasionally there is a delay and a little help needed to realise the perfection of the design. Sounds about right.*

CONCLUSION

Knowing yourself as the awareness
behind the voice is freedom.
Eckehart Tolle

So here we are at the end of the book. Has it all sounded absurd? Or has there been something here that has resonated with anything you know deep down to be true?

Let's look at the whole picture to see what changes as we see through to who we really are.

No experience of freedom

We could start perhaps with those moments when we have no experience of freedom. Maybe you have had them. Maybe this was why you picked up the book in the first place. I certainly have. These are the times when the insecure and terrified compulsions or voices in our head seem absolutely valid. When there is no recognition of any distinction between thought and reality. When there is no understanding that we or life or other people could be anything more than how it all looks right now. We seem trapped in inevitable reactions and knee jerks with no possibility of anything other, no choice at all. No freedom.

Wanting freedom

Then there may be moments when we come out of the mindless reactions and become more reflective. It looks to us that perhaps we do have an ability to choose. That perhaps other people choose more wisely. But no matter how hard we try, we just can't seem to make the choices we believe we should make.

We become exhausted from trying to change, from trying to be a better person or to get what we want in order to be secure and happy. We may want to drink less alcohol, take less drugs, shop less, play less video games, argue less, work more or work less or have fewer rituals or whatever other habit.

But the drinking, drugs, shopping, work rituals are a way of blanking the thoughts which blanks the feelings. In a very real sense, all these numbing behaviours are inevitable, sensible even.

When we think we have to feel better or manage our thoughts or mental state, we have no choice about whether we will fall into our numbing patterns. We can hold out for a while perhaps. But holding out against firmly held beliefs is limited, exhausting and temporary.

We beat ourselves up for the 'bad choices' we continue to make. And each bad choice we make seems to be more evidence that we are 'weak' or 'wrong'.

So we struggle on, blaming ourselves as though we could actually decide anything, as though we had any choice.

Glimpsing freedom

Then sometimes we notice a different experience. We may have the tiniest recognition that somehow we are more than the small self we believe ourselves to be.

There might be an idea or a nudge to do or say something and then insecure thinking takes over.

"You haven't got the staying power to do anything. Look at the mess you've made so far."

"People are laughing at you."

"You fail everything you attempt. Why bother?"

The love and intelligence of who we are is noticed but insecure thinking is believed. This thinking looks rational. It looks like it is keeping our feet on the ground and that seems safe and sensible.

This is the world of the declaration of love that goes unspoken, the soaring mission that never gets clearance for take off. We feel the prompt of life but we are still caught up in narrow beliefs about who we are, what we are capable of and what others think.

Knowing we are freedom

Then one day, who knows how, (maybe through something seen here), we come into the understanding that we are so much more than we think. We notice the space of awareness, love and peace and we know deep within that that space is who we are. We notice the doing and the not doing. All of it is perfect. We know that any thoughts about the reasons to act or not act, about whether this will make us happy or not, successful or not, a good person or not, loved or not are irrelevant.

We also notice the insecure thinking that appears. The thoughts telling us not to risk self or reputation, not to waste time and effort. From this space we love those thoughts, we notice they are acted on or not. It doesn't matter either way.

Now that we are coming from the inside, from where life originates, we have front row seats at the premiere of that amazing transition of formless to form. We can grab our bucket of popcorn and watch a problem, an opportunity, a lover, an enemy appear and disappear like a rabbit in a magician's hat. And all the while we remain aware.

And because we know we are the pure freedom of life, this belief we had of who and how we had to be dissolves into itself. We are freedom, love, joy and peace. We need nothing. There is nothing to do, no one to do anything and nowhere to get to. And the resolve and immersion in life from this space is immeasurable.

We are freedom. And now that freedom is paying the rent or moving house or writing a book or saying words or cuddling a child or standing for office or washing up or anything else.

Actions won't be coming from beliefs about what should or should not be done. They won't come from will power or determination. Or insecurity or control. Life will be happening because, once the beliefs and thoughts of who we are are no longer taken seriously, there is nothing in the way. It will happen because it cannot not happen.

As freedom itself, we change job or take someone to court or research a diagnosis or grieve a death. Every emotion is possible and allowed. Every outcome is possible and allowed. A court case, at one time only about division, can now be the expression of one being. A diagnosis, previously a source of panic, can now be the miracle of what we know to do. A death, once our worst fear, can confirm the impossibility of loss.

Pure life, freedom and love express themselves and in doing so magnify life, freedom and love.

Available to everything, there is no self to defend or prop up. There is no idea of who we are to restrict what life is capable of expressing. Vision and reach is infinite.

And then we forget. Of course we forget. We have to forget. And it looks like we are small and trapped and isolated and insecure. We believe this and we suffer.

And then we remember again. And each time we remember, we realise that the forgetting is just part of the design. And the forgetting becomes sweeter and more perfect until the suffering is no more.

It is all welcome.

We are space for it all. Life is unlimited.

We are free.

ACKNOWLEDGMENTS

Thank you.
To everyone who has pointed anyone
to unlimited life.
You know who you are.

There was a girl, let's call her Everygirl, who thought that she wasn't OK. She thought she was missing something. She felt lonely, scared, inadequate. She believed what she thought about who she was. She thought that there was something wrong with her. She thought that she had to avoid the things that were scaring her, hide herself behind make up and likes. She tried to get control of this life through food or approval or love or friends or exercise or good marks. She tried to blank out her mind with physical pain.

There was a boy, let's call him Everyboy, who thought that he wasn't OK. He thought he was missing something. He felt lonely, scared, inadequate. He believed what he thought about who he was. He thought there was something wrong with him. He thought these feelings he had weren't normal and had to be resisted and hidden. He thought life was all on his shoulders and that he had to hoard knowledge and take control so that the world would be less frightening. He withdrew into himself, hiding anyway in books or games. Or he battled it out in the playground or sports field, guns blazing, armour locked in place, fists clenched.

As Everygirl and Everyboy turned into adults they kept on and on trying to feel better, more secure, less wrong. All the places they looked to for solace told them that they were not normal, not right. They were told they should be controlling their mind, thinking good thoughts, that it is not OK to experience certain emotions. They were told to get their life sorted, to get their head fixed, to find what they needed.

Everygirl and Everyboy felt worse and worse. They felt as though their lives were falling apart. Everything looked impossible. Why did everyone else seem to have it all together? They dragged themselves through the rest of their days feeling inadequate, isolated, distant.

The End.

Really?

Is this what we want for Everygirl and Everyboy?

Is that what we want from this story, from any story? Surely there's got to be something else?

How about we make something different in this short eternal tale. How about at some stage – maybe even right from their time in the womb, or when they are babies or toddlers, or when they start school, or when they are teenagers, or playing sports, or staring their first job, or when they do a course with work, or when they go out with friends – Everygirl and Everyboy are told the truth?

This telling of the truth is no ordinary telling. This is a telling that is so connected, loving, authentic, joyful that it reaches deep inside Everygirl and Everyboy, beneath the layers of pain, frustration, disappointment, and holds what they have always known up to the light.

And in that telling and reaching and illumination everything changes.

The reality of this fearful inadequate self in this insecure world is seen for what it is. An illusion created from within, made of nothing. So fragile and inconsequential it collapses, disappears at the gentlest question.

The battle, the hiding, the striving, the avoiding, the resisting, the fighting, the overcoming are now bewildering. What was there ever to hide from or resist?

Reality has shifted. An entirely new life emerges from an entirely new self, a self that becomes less of itself every day as limits that never existed give way to possibility, openness, potential. Everygirl and Everybody realise they are nothing and they are the entire world.

Everygirl and Everyboy go about their lives with a transformed perspective, as awareness, completeness, love and freedom. Those moments when they feel heart breaking sadness or desperate insecurity are part of being alive. Those moments of utter joy and immense peace are there for the coming and going. There is nothing to close off from. Nothing to cling to. They can experience it all. Whatever it is, they welcome it.

They look around at their life. They know that somehow this noticing and appreciation is emerging through them, something is using them to experience this wealth of beauty and intricate detail. A breathtaking world of sights, sounds, smells and textures brought alive simply because Everygirl and Everyboy are alive. Their life is a celebration of the miracles that exist solely because they exist.

They notice the ideas that come to them from out of the blue. The words that appear on the page. The trajectory of a ball off their racket. The melodies that emerge. The colours that take shape on the canvas. Their entire selves relax in the knowledge that this is always there for them, there is nothing to control or coerce or manipulate. It is there. Simple, easy, obvious and utterly mind-blowing.

And they say it quietly.

Just two words. Words that are thrown out mindlessly at every cash register or muttered to every hand holding open a door.

Yet now these two words have the depth of the oceans, the grace and magnitude of the highest skies, the stampeding urgency of a wildebeest migration, the transparent, unguarded, heart-felt honesty of a baby's gaze.

Quietly they say it.

Thank you.

ABOUT THE AUTHOR

Clare Dimond works with individuals, schools, businesses and organisations exploring how excellence, freedom, love and creativity are our natural state.

For materials, resources, programmes or to ask any questions raised by this book, visit www.claredimond.com

ALSO BY CLARE DIMOND

REAL The Inside-Out Guide to Being Yourself

Made in the USA
Middletown, DE
29 September 2023